"I'm
the Kind
of Kid
Who..."

DEBBIE MILLER • EMILY CALLAHAN

"I'm the Kind of Kid Who..."

Invitations That Support Learner Identity and Agency

HEINEMANN
Portsmouth, NH

Heinemann

145 Maplewood Avenue, Suite 300

Portsmouth, NH 03801

www.heinemann.com

Library of Congress Cataloging-in-Publication Data

Names: Miller, Debbie, author. | Callahan, Emily, author.
Title: "I'm the kind of kid who …" : invitations that support learner
    identity and agency / Debbie Miller and Emily Callahan.
Identifiers: LCCN 2021054921 | ISBN 9780325132389
Subjects: LCSH: Decision making—Study and teaching. | Student-centered
    learning. | Choice (Psychology) | Identity (Psychology) | Agent (Philosophy)
Classification: LCC LB1062.5 .M55 2022 | DDC 153.8/3—dc23/eng/20220110
LC record available at https://lccn.loc.gov/2021054921

Editor: Zoë Ryder White
Production: Victoria Merecki
Cover and interior designs: Suzanne Heiser
Cover art: © happyvector071/stock.adobe.com (confetti),
          © Topuria Design/stock.adobe.com (envelope)
Typesetting: Gina Poirier, Gina Poirier Design
Manufacturing: Val Cooper

Printed in the United States of America on acid-free paper
1 2 3 4 5   CGB   26 25 24 23 22 PO 33995

To all the kids.
Every single one.

CONTENTS

ONLINE VIDEOS

To view these videos:

1. Go to http://**hein.pub/KindofKid-login**.

2. Log in with your username and password. If you do not already have an account with Heinemann, you will need to create an account.

3. On the Welcome page, choose "Click here to register an Online Resource."

4. Register your product by entering the code **KINDKID** (be sure to check the acknowledgment box under the keycode).

5. Once you have registered your product, it will appear alphabetically in your account list of My Online Resources.

Note: When returning to Heinemann.com to access your previously registered products, simply log into your Heinemann account and click on "View my registered Online Resources."

IN APPRECIATION

It is with gratitude and appreciation that we acknowledge those who have inspired and supported us in the beginning and along the way.

To Jude: Do you know you were the inspiration for this book? Thank you for being so clear with us about who you are and what you need. We can't wait for teachers to hear your story and learn from you!

To Haley Hurst (Jude's teacher) and Tricia DeGraff (executive director at the Academy for Integrated Arts in Kansas City, Missouri): We thank you for understanding the power of learning alongside children and believing in their brilliance.

To the kids in Emily's classes at Crossroads Academy-Quality Hill and Lillian Schumacher Elementary in the Liberty Public Schools: Thank you for being so willing to try out new things, reflect on what happened, and share what you've learned with us and the world. You and your stories are the heart of our book and we couldn't have made it without you!

To our friends and colleagues in the North Kansas City Public Schools: Thank you for bringing us together all those years ago. Who knew we'd become fast friends and eventually write a book together?

To our amazing team at Heinemann: We thank you for everything!

To Margaret LaRaia and Zoë Ryder White: How lucky are we to have had two such kind, smart, and thoughtful editors? (Very!) Margaret, thank you for listening to our early ideas and offering both freedom and guidance as we took those first steps. Zoë, thank you for gently and expertly guiding us to the finish—your "need to know" gave us clarity and empowered us to do and be our best.

Thank you to Krysten Lebel, editorial coordinator; Kim Cahill, marketing manager; and Victoria Merecki, production editor, for your exquisite attention to detail. And to our designer, Suzanne Heiser: Thank you for making our book so beautiful. We so appreciate how you honored and enhanced our vision.

And to our families and friends . . .

From Emily

To Debbie: I somehow knew after our initial meeting over a decade ago that we'd become close friends and that you'd continue to be my mentor. Thank you for asking me to partner with you on this book and for continuing to inspire me to try new things, ask more questions, and be more reflective. Thank you for your guidance and helping me see that I'm the kind of teacher who can figure things out.

To Matt Glover: Thank you for helping me understand the power of choice and what children are capable of as writers. And to Nicole Johnson, Lindsay Yates, Lacey Lewis, and Lisa Moss: Your check-ins, encouragement, and feedback were invaluable.

To Jeremy: Thank you for your unwavering love and support (and for being such a super dad during all those early morning Zooms with Debbie). And to my boys, Fletcher and Theo: Thank you for your love, hugs, and kisses that keep me going.

And to my mom, Nancy: It's because of you I became a teacher. Thank you for showing me the way and being the best model I could ever ask for. Thank you for always inviting me to try new things, for supporting all of my ideas, and for allowing me to figure out who I was.

From Debbie

To Emily: I can't think of anyone I'd rather write a book with than you! Your can-do spirit; those early, *early* morning Zoom calls; and all those Google Doc to-do lists were just what we needed to stay (mostly) on track! I can't wait for teachers to meet and learn from you and your kids—this ride with you has been magical.

To Don: Remember in another dedication when I said, "And now, my love, are we ready to play? Grab the snorkels, pack the shorts, and let's sail away for a year and a day"? I really, really mean it this time! (Book all the tickets.)

And to our boys, Noah and Chad: Thank you for everything! You and your families bring us so much love, happiness, and joy. We love love love you! (And you can come with us if you want . . .)

And finally, dear readers: We appreciate you! We hope you have as much fun reading our book as we did making it!

Love,
Debbie and Emily

INTRODUCTION

If a student can figure something out for him- or herself, explicitly providing the information preempts the student's opportunity to build a sense of agency and independence . . . being told what to do and how to do it—over and over again—provides the foundation for a different set of feelings and a different story about what you can and can't do, and who you are.

—**Peter Johnston,** *Choice Words: How Our Language Affects Children's Learning*

Meet Jude

I t's reading time in Haley Hurst's second-grade classroom, and children are reading, writing, and talking about books. A few teachers and I (Debbie) notice Jude in a corner, making what looks like a tower. Out of books. We exchange glances, our eyes sending signals that say, "What are they doing?" We watch the tower rise and fall, and rise and fall again, as Jude makes calculated adjustments each time. Jude is engaged in a delicate balancing act, books supporting books, reaching higher and higher (Figure I–1). We're mesmerized by this child and their tower, somehow knowing to keep quiet, stay back, and let them be.

It's taken me time to understand the why of keeping quiet and letting a child be. Our natural impulse is to interrupt, remind the child this is reading time right now, and we don't play with books. But what can happen when we resist our impulse to intervene and simply watch what the child does next? Instead of rushing forward to "make things right" in our own minds, what

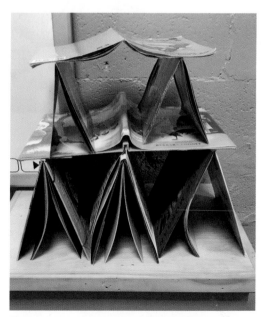

Figure I–1

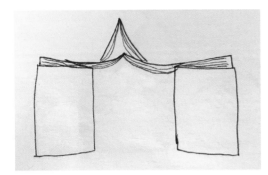

Figure I–2

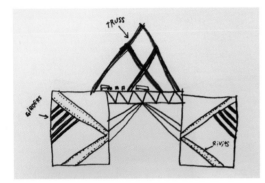

Figure I–3

Figure I–4

Figure I–5

might happen if we wait and see what the child does with their freedom? Jude's teachers and I stand waiting together as they continue—they're so absorbed in their work that they don't even notice us standing there.

Finally satisfied with their tower, Jude grabs a clipboard and a pencil, gets comfortable, and begins to draw (Figure I–2).

But Jude isn't done yet. They remove the drawing from the clipboard, turn it over, and begin anew, except this time Jude opens the book they've been reading, flips to the page they sticky noted the day before, and now uses a pen to make the art shown in Figure I–3. (See Figures I–4 and I–5 for the book Jude was reading.)

Teachers and I exchange glances again, this time mouthing words like *Wow!* and *What?* We can hardly contain ourselves, realizing we've just witnessed something extraordinary.

I make my way over to Jude and congratulate them on what a thinker they are.

"No. I'm not a thinker," they say, looking me straight in the eye. "I'm a builder. A doer. A maker of things."

"Ah," I say, "I'm sorry, Jude. I've got it now. Let me write that down in my notebook: you're a builder, a doer, a maker of things."

Jude nods, turns away, and carefully dismantles their tower.

The backstory: *We were in Jude's classroom as part of an ongoing lab project—students were immersed in a nonfiction study, and lab teachers and I were playing around with ways for children to show their thinking and learning. We thought about sticky notes, notebook entries, and creating a graphic organizer, but nothing seemed quite right for everyone. In the end, we asked ourselves this: "What if we left it up to them? What if we gave children the power to choose?" And that's just what we did—we simply asked, "How will you show your learning today? How will you show what you know? You might use your notebooks, sticky notes, chart paper, this organizer, or these large and small blank pieces of paper . . ."*

No limits.

We predicted many children would choose to use sticky notes or their notebooks—both were good, familiar options. But we were also hoping there might be some kids who would branch out this day and find another way. (Full disclosure: there were some doubts. Would things get messy? Would kids not know what to do? Would chaos ensue?)

No one needed to worry! Things weren't perfect, but they were good enough. And just think what we learned from Jude! They gave teachers and children a vision of what might be. This isn't about everyone building towers out of books.

It is about placing children in learning situations where they are free to make choices, discover, learn, and get to know more about who they are, how they learn, and what makes them happy.

Jude was all the buzz that day. Months later, I still think about them, share their story with any teacher who will listen, and wonder what they are up to now. But recently my fixation has shifted, and I've been working to figure out these two questions:

1. What is within Jude that we want for all children?

2. How can we ensure that every child in our care comes to understand more about who they are and how they learn and to believe in themselves the way Jude does?

The first question was the easy one. When I close my eyes and think back to that day, this is what I believe is within Jude:

- **Identity:** Jude has a sense of who they are and how they learn: "I'm a builder, a doer, a maker of things."

- **A sense of agency:** Jude believes they are the kind of kid who can figure things out: they know what they need to do and they have strategies they know they can use to do this— "I read, I know to mark what's most interesting to me with a sticky note, I can build, and I can draw to help me understand ideas."

- **Creativity and resourcefulness:** No blocks? No worries. "I'll use books."

- **Confidence:** Jude stands up for themself and understands it's OK to say no when someone—even a teacher—describes them in a way they disagree with: "No, I'm not a thinker . . ."

And the second question? What actions can we take to ensure that every child in our care comes to understand more about who they are and how they learn and to believe in themselves the way Jude does? The more I thought about it, the more I understood it really *is* all about choice. Jude built their tower in response to a simple question: How will you share your learning today? So . . . what if children were offered invitations—real in-an-envelope invitations—that encouraged them to make authentic choices that mattered to them? And then (we're not finished yet!), what if we taught them to reflect on the choice(s) they made: What happened? What did I learn? What do I know about what I need and how I learn that I didn't know before?

What if children were offered a whole range of invitations to choose? Across a school year? Could the power of choice and reflection help them understand more about who they are and how they learn? Maybe!

I couldn't wait to call my longtime friend and teacher extraordinaire Emily Callahan—would she be interested in trying this out with me? In her classroom with kids? I'd been working with her district for years, and we'd been learning together for many of them. I was pretty sure she'd say yes. (She did!) And now we can't wait to share with you what happened!

How Our Book Works

Section 1 (Chapters 1–3)

- **Chapter 1** explains more about invitations. What are they? How do they work?

- **Chapter 2** speaks to planning for invitations. What do we consider? How do we learn where children are and what they need?

- **Chapter 3** is about how invitations thrive in authentic, collaborative classrooms. How do children inspire, support, and sustain each other? How do we support them in their efforts?

Section 2 (Chapters 4–7)

These chapters are annotated photo essays describing four different invitations from start to finish. Each invitation is built around a predictable structure:

- **Getting started:** What might I need to know?

- **Planning:** What's the plan? How do we start?

- **Digging in:** What did we try? What happened? What did we learn?

- **Reflection:** Where are we now?

You might be thinking that Jude's story is an isolated one, that not many children have the confidence and self-awareness to speak their truth to an adult in such an honest and straightforward way. But after thirty years in my own classroom, and years of working with other teachers and their children since then, I'm convinced that when we give children opportunities to *practice* making choices that matter, when we promote authentic learning situations where they have daily opportunities to try things out and reflect on what happened and what they learned, all children have the capacity to develop learning identities, confidence, and a sense of agency.

Could it be that our classrooms are filled with many extraordinary children just waiting to be discovered? Children just waiting to discover themselves? Yes! In the pages that follow, I can't wait for you to meet Anthony and Atticus, Henry, Kendall, and so many of their friends! Here's a sneak peek (Figures I–6 to I–8)!

Figure I–6 ● To see how Anthony and Atticus explore a topic they care about, see Chapter 7, pages 132–133.

Figure I–7 ● To learn about Henry and Zoeyayn's plan for teaching first graders math, see Chapter 7, pages 140–143.

Figure I–8 ● To see how Kendall and other children make their thinking visible, see Chapter 6, pages 108–113.

Advancing Learner Identity and a Sense of Agency

When you change the way you look at things,
the things you look at change.

—Max Planck, *physicist*

Remember these two questions from the introduction?

- What is within Jude that we want for all children?
- How can we ensure that every child in our care comes to understand more about who they are and how they learn?

We have some ideas about what is within Jude, and now we're set to tackle the second question in more depth: How do we make what we want for all children a reality? What concrete actions can we take to awaken, nurture, and develop learner identity and a sense of agency that lives within them? Because as much as we might want to, we can't just "give" these things to children—there are no magic programs or potions to call upon. (Thank goodness!)

The truth is, children don't need magic—what they really need are invitations from their teachers to discover themselves *for* themselves, invitations that encourage them to find out even more about who they are, how they learn, and what they need to thrive.

What Is an Invitation?

Simply put, an invitation is a way to *invite* children to make their own choices in a variety of settings and learning situations in the classroom. We write the invitation's guiding question(s) on a note card and seal it in an envelope to open with children as an official way to dive in and build curiosity and excitement. Kids wonder, "Who will open it? What will it say?"

Similar to the provocations that are part of Reggio Emilia classrooms as well as the Story Workshop process described by Susan Harris MacKay (2021), invitations promote student choice, collaborative opportunities, and full access

1

to the learning environment. Both approaches center children and nurture experimentation, problem-solving, and discovery.

Centering children doesn't mean we're about hands-off teaching, that we're stepping down, handing over our responsibilities, leaving everything to chance. It's really the opposite—we're stepping up when we believe in children's capabilities, release control, and create conditions and structures that honor and support them in their efforts. Sometimes we hesitate to do this because we aren't sure that children will make good choices; we may think they're not quite ready. But they're ready whenever we are! Remember, it isn't as much about the choice as it is about the process: *What did I try? What happened? What did I learn?* It's the whole of the experience that allows children to grow into themselves and figure out what works for them. And what doesn't.

What does "grow into themselves" mean? Here's an example: In one third-grade classroom, kids were digging into this invitation: *What if you could choose where you want to learn and work?* They tried out different workspaces over a couple of weeks during reading time, thinking through their purpose each day (Figures 1–1 and 1–2): *What am I going to do today? What kind of space do I think I need to do that?* Each day after reading time, children reflected on what they'd tried, what happened, and what they'd learned about themselves. In just couple of weeks kids were able to make decisions like these:

Figure 1–1

Figure 1–2

(For more info on this invitation, check out Chapter 4.)

- "I'm starting a new book today, so I need a quiet spot."

- "Our group needs a place to spread out all our stuff today, so we're going to work in the meeting area."

- "I'm feeling kind of grumpy today. I need an out-of-the-way spot where I can work through it on my own or maybe with a friend."

- "My partner and I need a place where we can do some research and talk today, so we're going to go over to the little table by the door, so we won't bother anybody."

- "Our book club is meeting today, so we've booked a table in the library."

Real-World Invitations

The choices invitations offer mirror the kinds of decisions people make in the world—from choosing what to read, to investigating something they truly care about, invitations invite children to assume more responsibility for their learning and teachers to let them.

The invitations in this book focus on four areas for choice making (Figure 1–3):

- space
- materials
- what readers do in the world
- what to learn about and how to share it.

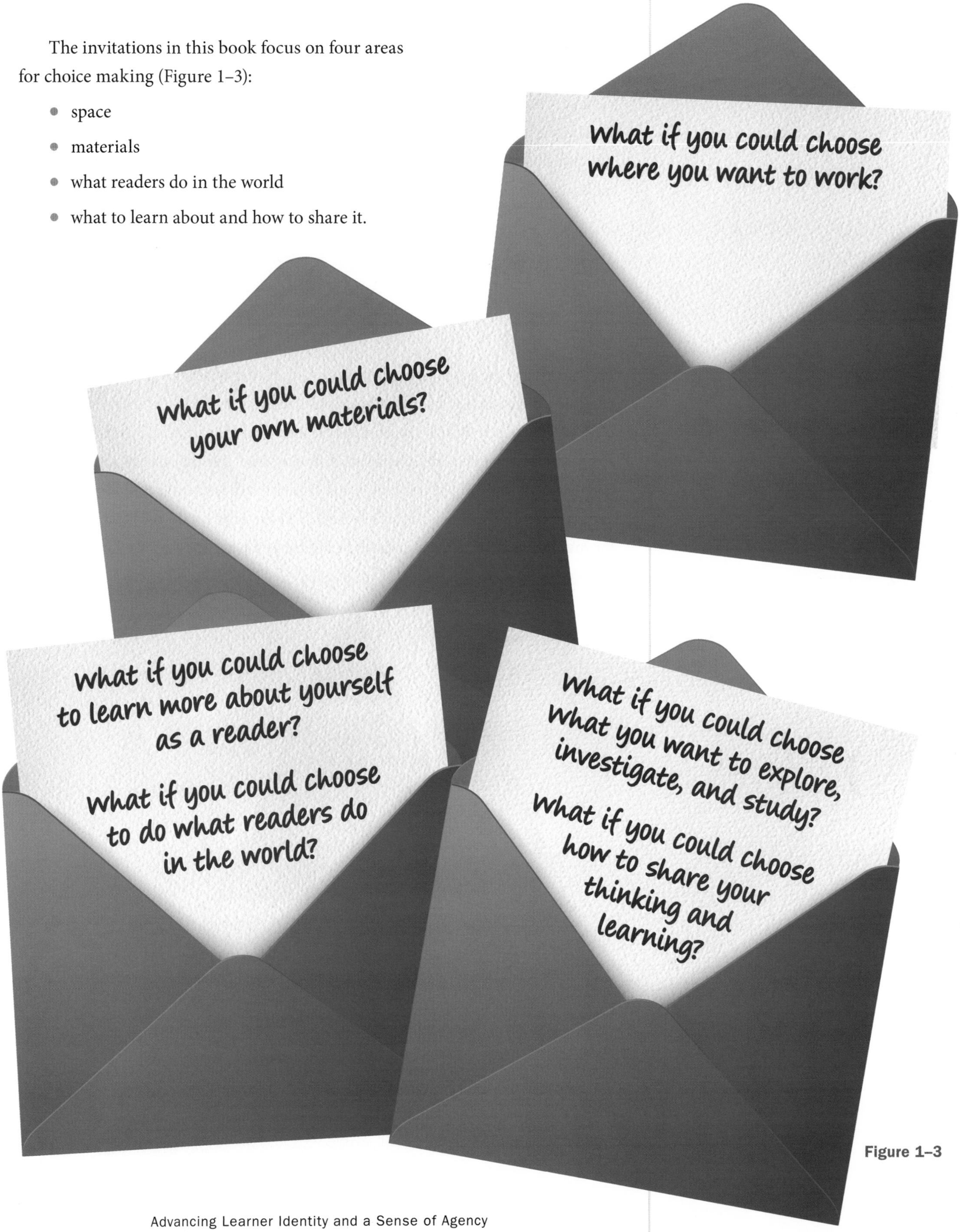

What if you could choose where you want to work?

What if you could choose your own materials?

What if you could choose to learn more about yourself as a reader?

What if you could choose to do what readers do in the world?

What if you could choose what you want to explore, investigate, and study?

What if you could choose how to share your thinking and learning?

Figure 1–3

Invitations are loosely organized by levels of sophistication, though there's no set order. You can jump in anywhere! But depending on children's experiences, the invitations about materials and space are a good place to begin if children haven't had opportunities to make these choices yet. These early invitations support the others and offer opportunities for kids to experience making choices and reflecting on their decisions early in the year.

When Do Invitations Fit Within the Day and Across the Year?

Invitations are meant to support purposeful, in-depth learning—they're not taught in isolation nor are they an end in themselves. That's why invitations are most often offered within the context of other learning: reading, writing, math, social studies, science, or a designated choice time. Invitations are a means to a deeper understanding of content (what students are learning) and identity and agency (who they are and how they learn). There aren't hard and fast timelines for invitations, though you can see in Figure 1–4 how once an invitation is

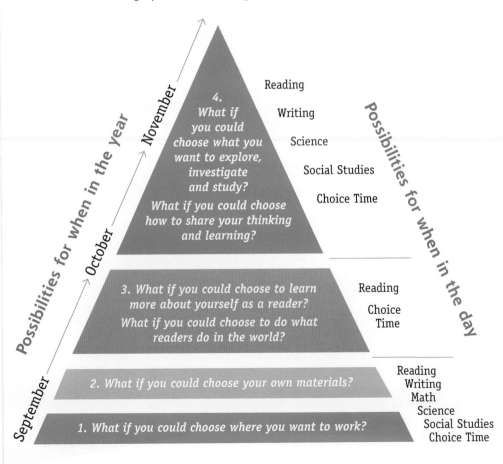

Figure 1–4

Possibilities for when in the year

Possibilities for when in the day

November

October

September

4.
What if you could choose what you want to explore, investigate and study?
What if you could choose how to share your thinking and learning?

Reading

Writing

Science

Social Studies

Choice Time

3. *What if you could choose to learn more about yourself as a reader?*
What if you could choose to do what readers do in the world?

Reading

Choice Time

2. *What if you could choose your own materials?*

Reading
Writing
Math
Science
Social Studies
Choice Time

1. *What if you could choose where you want to work?*

offered, it continues to evolve over time and across the year—one invitation layers into another.

In general, it makes sense to launch the invitations about space and materials in September, the invitations about book choice and making thinking visible in October, and the invitations to choose what to learn and how to share it around December. But it doesn't have to be that way. You might want to start with kids choosing books they want to read. It's up to you and what you think would most benefit the children in front of you.

If you have mandates or restrictions in one subject area, is there another that's less restrictive? We don't know any programs or mandates that prohibit inviting children to choose where they'll work, who they'll work with, or the materials they use. (And we hope you don't either!) Even within a mandated program, there are opportunities for student choice.

You may be wondering about the references to "choice time." Emily and I define it as at least a thirty-minute block of time where children are able to choose what they're working on. When possible, we offer invitations within subject areas, but sometimes teachers get caught in the middle—you want to try something new, but you aren't able to be as flexible as you'd like. No worries! You still have options! And designating at least thirty minutes a day for choice time is one of them.

But before we go on the lookout for those minutes, let's think about what choice time has to offer:

- If you're unable to launch invitations within subject areas, they can all be offered during choice time.

- Even if you're able to offer invitations within subject areas, choice time can be powerful for you and your kids too—during this time children can choose to continue the work they've started in subject areas, allowing more time for in-depth personal investigations, student-led book clubs, and more independent reading and writing with choice of text for readers and genre for writers.

- Choice time is unstructured, offering children time to explore and investigate anything they are interested in. Sometimes units "rule the learning," and this time gives children opportunities to make choices about topics they want to investigate and explore in addition to unit work.

Are you curious about choice time but not sure you can fit it into your day? We understand. Every minute is precious, and there are too few of them as it is.

But take a close look at your daily schedule—can you find some wiggle room? There are some things you can't change, but are there some you can? What about:

- Morning work? (What if you converted those minutes into choice time?)

- Whole-class trips to the bathroom and the long lineup for drinks? (What if you created a plan with kids about leaving the room when they need to? That's ten or so minutes twice a day—twenty minutes total.)

- Calendar time? (What if you placed it in math? Or shortened/ eliminated it? There's fifteen or so found minutes right there!)

- Packing up to go home? (Streamline it and gain 10–15 minutes.)

- What else?

Put those minutes together somewhere/anywhere in the day. Now you're set to offer kids authentic opportunities to learn more about themselves and each other as learners! Every single day. (We're not saying that some of these activities aren't important. But are they more important than advancing children's learner identities and their sense of agency?)

How Do Invitations Work?

Once you've offered an invitation, and children have made their choices and tried them out, don't just move on to something else. Having an experience doesn't mean children have learned from it! That's why reflection—asking children to think back to process what just happened—is essential to advancing learner identity and a sense of agency. You're asking children to be meta-cognitive, to develop an ongoing awareness of their thinking and learning and themselves as thinkers and learners.

Encouraging reflection across the school day normalizes it, making it something kids do naturally. "This is what learners do in school and in the world and this is what we do too." Naming what works for them helps the learning stick, making it more likely children will remember the strategy when a similar situation arises: "Oh! I remember when this happened before—I'm going to try that and see if it works for me again."

That's why these three questions are key—they place the child back into the experience and offer a straightforward structure that sparks a reflective stance:

- *What did I try?*
- *What happened?*
- *What did I learn?*

Asking children, "What will you try?" helps set just the right tone—it frees children to explore, experiment, and figure out what works for them and what doesn't, sending the message, "There's no pressure here, this is about learning about what works for you."

There will be (and should be!) missteps along the way. This is how we all learn! But every misstep serves as a step forward for everyone, because now we know more about ourselves than we did before. Think about the power in that for a child—understanding that mistake making isn't a bad thing, it's an opportunity to learn and grow. And that when we do make mistakes, it means that we're the kind of kids who challenge ourselves, take risks, and aren't afraid to fail. For more on mistake making, check out *Risk, Fail, Rise: A Teacher's Guide to Learning from Mistakes,* by M. Colleen Cruz (2020).

When you give children time to try things out, you'll hear them reflect in ways that sound like this:

Figure 1–5

- "I tried writing my thinking on a sticky note, but I didn't have enough room. I'm going to try one of those big sticky notes next time, or maybe a half-sheet of paper."

- "I used to read hard books, like chapter books. But today I tried reading some Elephant and Piggie books. Reading was so fun and I learned I like funny books, and even if books are easy to read, they can be good for me. And I love speech bubbles! They make me think about what I would say if I was in the story. I'm going to read all of them!"

Figure 1–6

- "I keep losing my stuff. I'm going to try using one of those tubs and keep all my things I need in there. Like my stick notes and markers and pencils and books. It'll be like my office so wherever I go, I can take my stuff with me."

- "Poetry is hard for me. Like today I was reading a poem in the book, *Words with Wings,* and I didn't get it at all. But then I remembered when this happened to me another time, I read the whole poem first, just to get the gist of it. Then I reread the stanzas and made notes about what I was thinking after each one. I tried it and it helped me again!"

- "You know how I like to talk all the time? I know I talk to help me figure things out but I can't always talk to someone, like maybe it's during a read-aloud. So I tried making a little notebook to use during read-alouds and write my thinking in it and I'm going to do it all the time now" (Figures 1–5 to 1–7).

Figure 1–7

Through reflection, kids develop an "agentive stance." They build a collection of strategies they can count on when similar situations arise or they get stuck. They develop an understanding of how they learn and what they need to do to figure things out. It takes time for children to view themselves as the kind of kids who make decisions, solve problems, and believe in themselves the way Jude does. But it's not a long, drawn-out process! That's because each day builds on those that have come before; every day a child has the chance to learn a little more about who they are and how they learn and how it feels to grow. And one of the best parts? They're not alone! A whole community of kids (and a teacher) are learning and growing right alongside them (Figure 1–8).

Every day children and teachers have opportunities to learn a little bit more about who they are as learners and what they need. It's a process, this ongoing awareness of self. We come to embrace the whole of who we are, acknowledging our strengths and struggles, and learning over time and experience how to manage both. Discovering who we are as learners is important, sometimes messy work, but it gives us the knowledge, the power, and the freedom to navigate the complexity of our lives, in and out of school.

Tried-and-True Reflective Questions for Kids and Teachers

Questions for Kids	Questions for Teachers
What did I learn about myself as a reader, writer, mathematician, historian, scientist, artist, kid today?	What did I learn about myself as a teacher today?
What's something new I tried today? What happened? What did I learn?	What's something new I tried today? What happened? What did I learn?
What did I learn today? How did I learn it?	What did I learn about a child today?
What choices worked best for me today?	What on-the-spot choices worked best for me today?
What problems do/did I have? What will/did I do? Do I need some ideas from others?	What problems did I have today? What will/did I do? Do I need some ideas from my kids or colleagues?
Did I surprise myself today? What happened?	Did I surprise myself today? What happened?
Did I help someone grow today? Did someone help me? How did that feel?	How did I help children grow today? How did they help me? How did that feel?

Figure 1–8

2

Planning for Invitations

If you have the end in view of . . . children learning certain set lessons, to be recited to a teacher, your discipline must be devoted to that result. But if the end in view is the development of a spirit of social cooperation and community life, discipline must grow out of and be relative to such an aim.

—John Dewey, *The School and Society*

This chapter is about planning for invitations in ways that center children, giving them the time, space, and support they need to discover more about who they are and how they learn. First, Emily thinks through a series of questions to help her make an initial, overarching plan, and second, she concentrates on a few specific actions that will help her find out where kids are and what they need once the invitation unfolds. But first things first. The last thing we want is for invitations to feel like a lot of extra work. There are things for you to think through, but truly, offering invitations to children shouldn't make you feel apprehensive or anxious. The whole point is offering children opportunities to make choices they haven't been invited to make before. That's it!

We'll share some background knowledge about the kind of thinking we do to plan, and we've included Emily's tried-and-true plans for each invitation in Section 2, all ready for you to use as is or to adapt to better meet the needs of your kids.

Remember there is no one way. Choose an invitation and give it a try! Then reflect: What happened? What did I learn about my kids and myself? What might be next for us? Because this really is all about making it your own—be who you are, not who you think you should be. Take all the time and space you need. You have a say.

Planning for Invitations: The Questions We Ask

Planning for an invitation doesn't need to take a lot of time—a solid 15–20 minutes is just about right. These are five questions Emily asks to guide her:

1. Why does this invitation matter?

2. What books, resources, and materials will children need?

3. When in the day will I launch it?

4. What will I say?

5. What reflective questions will I ask?

6. How will I know what kids need and how they're growing throughout the invitation? How will I communicate with them what I've learned?

1. Why Does This Invitation Matter?

How will this invitation help children discover more about who they are, how they learn, and what they need? Understanding why the invitation matters and how it can advance children's learning identities and their sense of agency provides purpose and clarity to the invitation and will help you think through the next steps.

One way to understand more about why an invitation matters is to try it out yourself before offering it to children. Doing the same work you're asking children to do grounds you in the invitation and gives you:

- confidence (I know what I'm talking about!)

- credibility (Students will know that I've done this work, too, and I understand what I'm asking them to do.)

- opportunities to identify pitfalls. (Ah! This was tricky for me, kids may need extra support here too.)

When you engage in the invitation in the same way you're asking kids to do, it adds personal perspective and depth to your interactions with children—you're able to model, think aloud, guide, and contribute in authentic ways during minilessons, conferences, small-group work, and casual, on-the-fly conversations.

The work you do doesn't have to be perfect, and you don't have to have all the answers. (No one does!) It's doing the work and naming what you did that matter most.

Here's an example of how Emily "did her own assignment" while thinking through the invitation *What if you could choose to learn more about yourself as a reader?* Emily read the article "Trampoline Trouble," made her thinking visible, and reflected and named what she did on the attached sticky note. She may or may not share her work with children, it's getting in touch with her process that matters most (Figure 2–1).

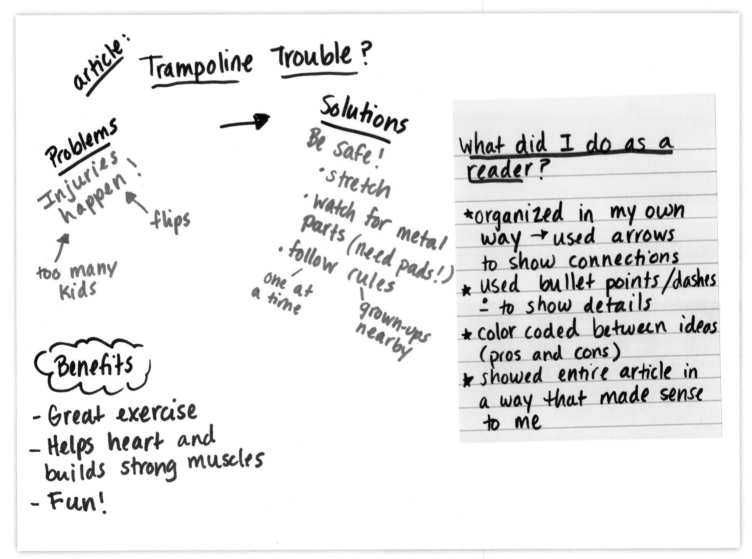

Figure 2–1

2. What Books, Resources, and Materials Will Children Need?

Are there things your children will need in addition to what is available? What about books? Materials? Other resources?

Invitations don't require many out of the ordinary requirements—all kids really need is access to a well-stocked supply area that include a variety of pencils, pens, markers, sticky notes, and different sizes and kinds of paper for children to choose from (Figure 2–2). And of course, wide access to books and other reading materials.

3. When in the Day Will I Launch It?

When in the day does this invitation fit best? Invitations are flexible! They can be launched in almost any subject area. The important part is to think it through—when in the day do you believe the invitation will be a natural fit? In what learning situation does this opportunity for choice feel most authentic? Will it be reading, writing, math, science, social studies, choice time, or somewhere else?

Here are a few scenarios:

- Launching the invitations about materials and space during choice time makes sense because they apply to all subject areas—kids are invited to choose the materials they'll need and where to work throughout the day, giving them a variety of settings and situations to learn about spaces that work and those that don't. If you don't have a choice time, any subject area will work!

- Inviting children to choose books they want to read makes sense in reading, but if that's not possible, you could also offer this invitation in choice time, or anytime in the day when all children can participate.

- Choosing what to learn about and how to share it could be launched in reading, social studies, science, or choice time. And if time is short, remember that choice time can provide extra time to research and work on/finish projects.

Whenever you choose to launch an invitation, keep in mind it can often transfer to other subject areas. Say you decide to launch the invitation *What if you could choose to do what readers do in the world?* in reading. Can you envision children applying that in social studies or science too?

Figure 2–2

4. What Will I Say?

This isn't about writing out a word for word script (unless you want to). If you do, it's not something to read aloud to kids or try to memorize. You do it to imagine yourself in the moment—If your kids were in front of you right now, what would you most want them to know about this invitation? What words or phrases will you use that center them instead of you? Then go back in and look for what's most important and write it on a sticky note so you'll remember. When you take the time to think about what to say, you'll feel clear, confident, calm, and ready to go (Figures 2–3 and 2–4). And so will your kids!

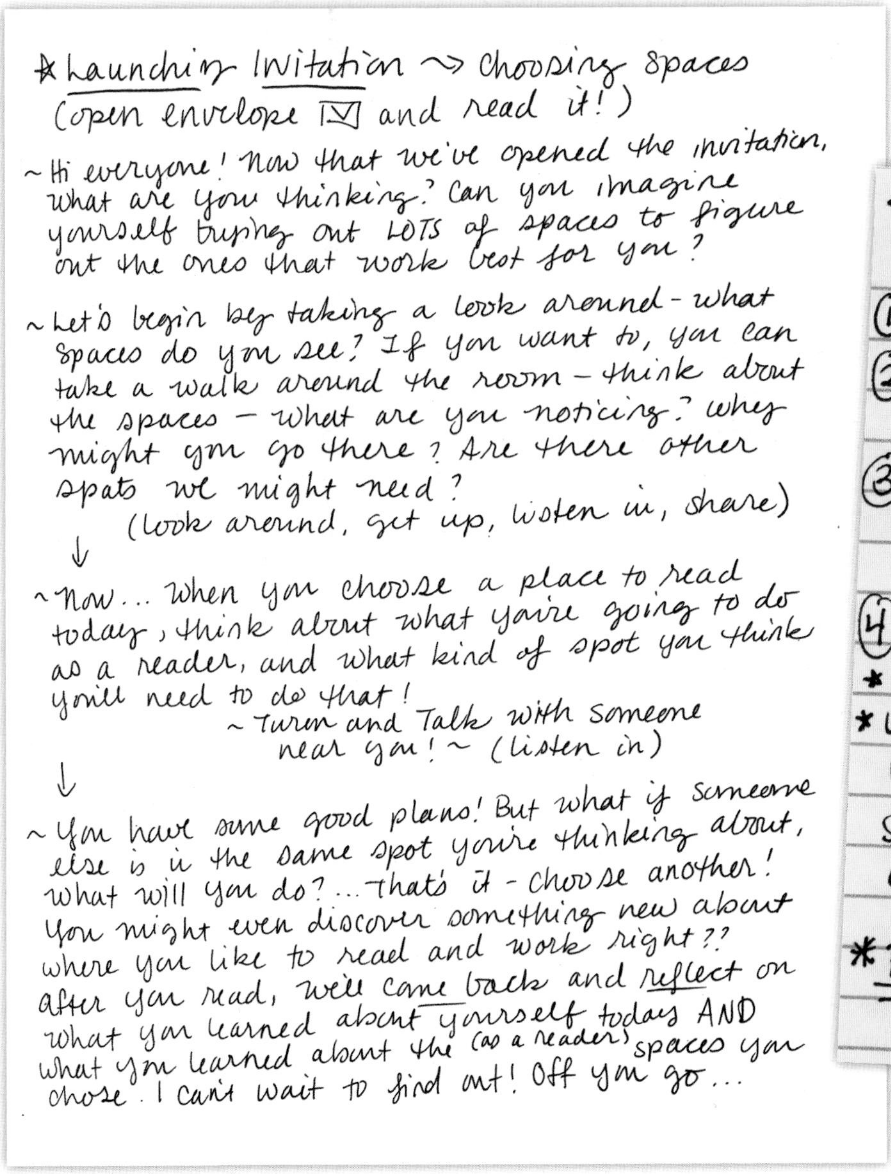

▼ Here's an example of a quick-write and sticky-note list Emily made to launch the first invitation: "What if you could choose where you want to work?"

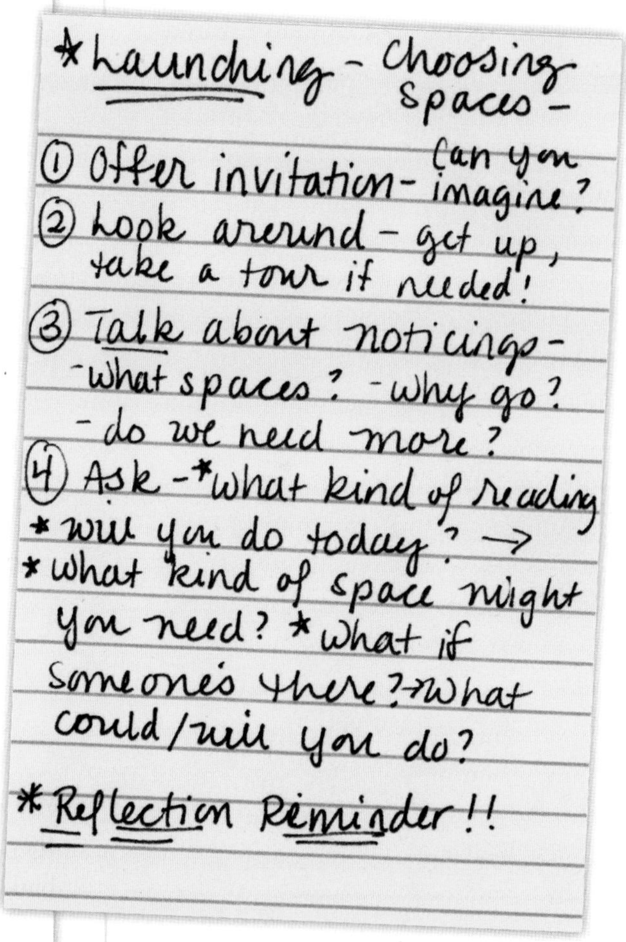

*Launching Invitation → Choosing Spaces
(open envelope ☑ and read it!)

~ Hi everyone! Now that we've opened the invitation, what are you thinking? Can you imagine yourself trying out LOTS of spaces to figure out the ones that work best for you?

~ Let's begin by taking a look around - what spaces do you see? If you want to, you can take a walk around the room - think about the spaces - what are you noticing? Why might you go there? Are there other spots we might need?
(look around, get up, listen in, share)
↓

~ Now... when you choose a place to read today, think about what you're going to do as a reader, and what kind of spot you think you'll need to do that!
~ Turn and Talk with someone near you! ~ (listen in)
↓

~ You have some good plans! But what if someone else is in the same spot you're thinking about, what will you do?... That's it - choose another! You might even discover something new about where you like to read and work right?? After you read, we'll come back and reflect on what you learned about yourself today (as a reader) AND what you learned about the spaces you chose. I can't wait to find out! Off you go...

Figure 2–3

*Launching - Choosing Spaces -

① Offer invitation - can you imagine?
② Look around - get up, take a tour if needed!
③ Talk about noticings - what spaces? - why go? - do we need more?
④ Ask - *what kind of reading *will you do today? → *what kind of space might you need? *what if someone's there? What could/will you do?

*Reflection Reminder!!

Figure 2–4

Whatever your process is for thinking through what you'll say when launching an invitation, it's important to be who you are, say what you mean, and show how you feel. There's vulnerability in this work—you can't know what will happen, and kids can't know either. Let them know this! And think about it this way: Don't you think embracing the unknown will make your teaching life a little more interesting? A bit more stimulating? A lot more real?

When you think about what you'll say, or reflect on what you said afterward, ask yourself:

- Who does the language I use center?

- How often do I say the word *I*?

- How often do I say *you*? *We*? *Us*?

Language such as that shown in Figure 2–5 centers children and transfers our power to them. Being prepared with a few standard phrases can be helpful as you work to let kids know that you want, need, and value their ideas.

5. What Reflective Questions Will I Ask?

Remember these reflective questions from Chapter 1?

- What did I learn about myself as a reader, writer, mathematician, historian, scientist, artist, kid today?

- What's something new I tried today? What happened? What did I learn?

- What did I learn today? How did I learn it?

- What choices worked best for me today?

- What problems do/did I have? What will/did I do? Do I need some ideas from others?

- Did I surprise myself today? What happened?

- Did I help someone grow today? Did someone help me? How did that feel?

They're a good place to start, and of course you'll have other questions you'll want to ask, too. Asking children to reflect on what happened and what they learned increases the likelihood their learning will stick, helping them build a repertoire of skills, strategies, and actions that become part of who they are and how they learn.

Don't wait until the end to ask children to reflect—these daily queries help children reflect (on their own or with others) on what they're noticing and learning all along the way.

Language That Centers Children

When We Say	Children Hear
"What are you thinking?"	My teacher cares about what we think. She listens to us and sometimes she even writes what we say in her notebook so she'll remember.
"What do you imagine?"	It's OK to dream in here! We don't have to rush. We can think about what we want to do and be.
"What else? Say more about that . . ."	My teacher believes I am a thinker. She knows I have more to say even when I don't think I do.
"I wonder if . . ."	My teacher doesn't think she knows everything. She wonders about things too. And if she has an idea for us, she doesn't tell us we have to do it. She is just wondering if we think it's a good idea.
"Who has another idea?"	My teacher isn't looking for "right answers." She wants to find out what everyone thinks because we think in all kinds of different ways. And all the ways matter.
"What will you try now?"	I can try out a lot of things to figure out what is just right for me. And just because you try one thing and it works doesn't mean you don't try something else.
"Ah! I hadn't thought about it like that before!"	I can help my teacher see things in a new way!
"Can you imagine yourself doing this? Think a minute about what you'll try first." **(Giving children time to think on their own and with others serves as a rehearsal for what's to come, giving them a place to begin.)**	I get to decide for myself what to try first, and so does everyone else. Imagining helps me think about what I want to try, so I'm not standing around, wondering what to do.
"Do you need any help?"	My teacher asks me if I need help and I can say, "Yes, please," "No, thank you," or "Not right now."

Figure 2–5

6. How Will I Know What Kids Need and How They're Growing Through the Invitation? How Will I Communicate with Them What I've Learned?

The best way to learn about what kids need and how they're growing is to watch what they do, listen to what they say, look closely at what they make, and confer with them to learn more. This is formative assessment at its finest! When you put all you've learned together, you'll have a clear picture of where kids are in the here and now, as well as a deeper awareness of how children are growing, both individually and as a class. (We'll be thinking more about these teacher actions on the following pages.)

When it comes to sharing with children what you've learned, it's an ongoing, everyday process! In addition to verbal acknowledgments during reflection and share time, conferences, and in-the-moment comments, Emily writes personal, handwritten notes to children throughout the invitations—this is yet another way for you to show children you see and hear them. These notes don't have to be fancy—even a sticky note will do! Think about when you get a handwritten note from someone whose opinion you value—How does it make you feel? And don't you wish you received more? (See Figures 2–6 to 2–10.)

Figures 2–6 to 2–10 ● Without Emily even knowing what kids were doing, some kept her notes in a notebook!

Planning for What Kids Need After the Invitation Is Launched

We look to kids for answers. Emily says, "I'm always on the lookout." And it's true! On any given day you'll find her, notebook at the ready, observing children, taking notes on what she's wondering and learning. Maybe she's on the lookout for new invitations, maybe she's assessing where children are and what they need next, or maybe she's curious about something else. Whatever her reason, she centers children by looking to them for answers. (You'll find examples of Emily's notes in Section 2.)

Emily makes it look easy, but it takes practice and resolve to slow down, be still, and focus our attention exclusively on children, even for just a few minutes! We all can get so caught up in "doing" that we forget to look to the children in front of us for guidance.

We come to understand what kids need (individually and collectively) when we use a combination of authentic, down-to-earth strategies like these:

- Watch what kids do.

- Listen to what kids say.

- Look closely at what kids make.

- Confer to listen and learn more.

Watch What Kids Do

Popularized by Yetta Goodman (1985), "kidwatching" is "watching kids with a knowledgeable head," allowing kids to inform their teachers about where they are, what they know, and what they need to grow. Kidwatching doesn't take a lot of time (just a few minutes), yet it yields significant big picture results, especially when done over a few days in a variety of settings.

When you observe children going about their learning, your goal is to be objective and open-minded, noting first what the child is doing without speculation or judgment, then using what you see to try to figure out intent. It's easy to jump to conclusions, but kidwatching is all about observing kids with genuine curiosity and a sense of not knowing. (Remember Jude and their tower of books?)

Except for maybe a nod and a smile, you're not engaging with children during this time, you're standing back, notebook in hand, being still and

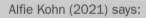

Alfie Kohn (2021) says:

"Teachers who listen to kids' conversations, observe their projects, and read their writing don't need to use tests. But this assumes kids have a chance to converse, design projects, and write. If they just listen to lectures and do worksheets, there's not much authentic learning to BE assessed."

focusing—What do you see? What do you notice? What do you wonder? (Jot it down so you can remember and reflect on what happened later.)

Resist the temptation to jump in and fix things. Relax! Kidwatching is all about learning. And the information is just for you.

Listen to What Kids Say

Listening in to what kids say is similar to kidwatching—you're taking a seeking-to-understand stance here, too. But instead of standing back, you're in the midst of things now, sitting at their level if possible, listening in and writing the gist of what you hear and notice as children talk, think, and learn together with partners and/or in small groups (Figure 2–11). You're not engaging much with children at this time, either. Your goal is the same as it is with kidwatching—you're listening in without speculation or judgment, using what you hear to figure out intent to inform your teaching decisions.

Let kids in on what you're doing and why before you begin kidwatching and listening in. Explain how you're taking a bit of time to learn more about them so you can be a better teacher. (This is another way to let kids know you see and hear them!)

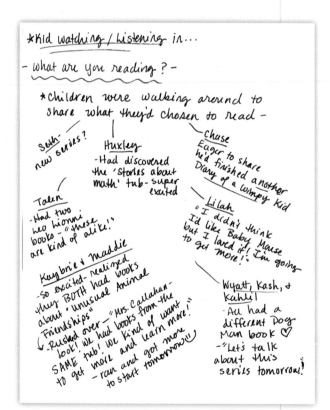

Figure 2–11 Emily's notes: kidwatching and listening in

Look Closely at What Kids Make

Looking closely at how children choose to make their thinking and learning visible will help you learn more about what's important to them, the mental processes they use to make meaning, how they hold onto their thinking, and what this means for next steps. "Looking at student work for evidence of student thinking more than correctness provides more actionable information for both teaching and learning" (Brookhart and Oakley 2021).

When you look at their work, think:

- What am I noticing?
- What surprised me?
- What has one child made that could inspire others?
- What patterns do I see in children's work that suggests new invitations, whole-group and small-group minilessons, or individual conferences?

There's a difference between looking at work that's formulaic and work where children have chosen how to make their thinking and learning visible. Worksheets and teacher-made organizers don't really give us much of anything to study—they're more about whether a child "got it" or didn't. That's why inviting children to show what they know in their own way teaches us so much more (Figures 2–12 and 2–13).

Confer to Listen and Learn More

Children aren't all in the same place at the same time. Conferring allows opportunities to differentiate/personalize invitations (and teaching) by offering children what they need then and there, on the spot. On-the-spot invitations are less formal than whole-group invitations and are offered in the moment, when you're working with a child (or children) and recognize a chance to offer an invitation that specifically addresses something that meets their needs in the moment. These invitations have a try-it-out kind of feel—"I'm noticing . . . and I wonder if this might be something to try?" And then it's the child who makes the call.

There are at least two kinds of on-the-spot invitations:

- **Mini-invitations that live within the larger one.** Let's say that you've launched an invitation that invites children to choose the math materials they need, and you notice one child connects with the invitation right away. She's even started teaching other kids some of her strategies for using materials in unique ways. An invitation to this child might be *What if you offered a series of short, small-group classes one or two days a week where you could teach others about some of your strategies during math? Kids could signup? What do you think? Do you want to give it a try?*

- **Offer a completely different invitation that meets the here-and-now needs of this child, this partnership, or this small group of children.** Let's say in this conference you learn the child sincerely wants to read two or three books at one time, but is having trouble keeping them all straight. An invitation to this child might be *What if when you're finished reading one of your books for the day, you could take a minute to write on a sticky note, or in your little pink notebook, what's happening and/or maybe a question? Write just enough so you can jump back in and know where you left off? What do you think? Do you want to give it a try?*

On-the-spot invitations aren't meant to be exclusive—if other children are intrigued and want to try it out too, the response is always, "Of course you can! And you might want to go talk with . . . to learn more. And you know I'm always happy to help."

Figure 2–12

Figure 2–13

3

Living in Caring and Collaborative Communities Where Learners and Learning Thrive

For me, the child is a veritable image of becoming, of possibility, poised to reach towards what is not yet, towards a growing that cannot be predetermined or prescribed. I see her and I fill the space with others like her, risking, straining, wanting to find out, to ask their own questions, to experience a world that is shared.

—Maxine Greene, *Commencement Address*

As children come to know more about who they are and what they need as learners, they're simultaneously coming to know more about their friends and how *they* learn and developing a collective sense of identity and agency. This isn't about homogeneity—it doesn't mean everyone thinks, dreams, or believes the same things. It is about children understanding they are part of something greater than themselves, that collectively they are braver, stronger, more able to do big things, more able to stand up for what's right, than they could do alone.

Invitations Are for Everyone!

It's important to say that invitations are for everyone. Think about the kids who are routinely told to sit up front or off to the side, "to stay out of trouble," so "I can keep an eye on you," or even "so you won't be distracted." What kinds of messages are we sending to them? What are the rest of the kids to think? This is about equity. Our mission is to engage all children in learning more about what they need to feel their best and be their most engaged and happy selves. Everyone has a say.

Children who act out can be the very ones who thrive when given the same opportunities and support for choice making as everyone else. When we're patient and consistent in our interactions with every child, they (and the rest of the kids) come to view themselves—one and all—as vital, contributing members of the community, and that feels good for everyone. How we view children sets the tone for how children view themselves and each other—this is where our power lives.

Invitations aren't something children earn and we never take them away as a consequence for challenging behavior. They're for everyone, always. What's our stance when things go wrong? Let's imagine a child's plan doesn't work out the way she thought it would—say she loses her way and begins to play around, act silly, distract others. What then? Do we resign ourselves and say this child, or even this class, isn't yet ready to make important choices? We hope not. But what do we do? In situations like these, it's time for us to step in. Not to scold the child or blame ourselves, but to own the situation, stay calm in the moment, and ask the child something like this, "What are you working to do? What happened? How can I help? Let's figure this out together." Maybe this means you and the child make a new plan, figure out new strategies, find a new spot . . . and then make a new plan to try.

That's what happened with two children in the midst of a sea turtle study. Emily noticed they were distracted and decided to step in and see what she could learn. Her conferring notes (Figures 3–1 to 3–4) tell the story—they'd done a lot of work already, but were uncertain about how to move forward on their own: "Could you help us stay on track?" (She could!) They created a to-do list with Emily, and it wasn't long before they were back on the rails!

And really, nothing is lost for the child or the teacher. We're taking responsibility. We're trying to make things better. We're growing as teachers and humans. And we're showing this child, and any child nearby who is listening, this is who we are, this is what we believe, this is what they can expect from us. And hopefully, this is the kind of thinking they'll come to also expect from themselves and each other.

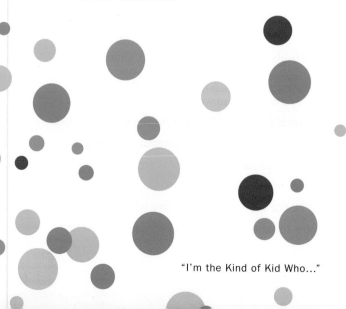

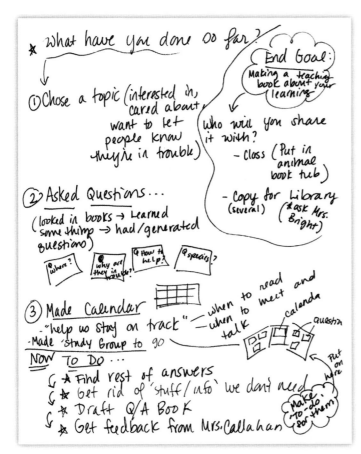

Figure 3–1

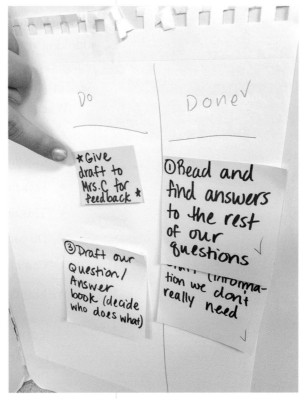

Figure 3–2

Figure 3–3

Figure 3–4

The Intentional Use of Language

Kids mirror what we say and do, and what we don't. The more we think aloud and make our thinking visible to them, the more likely children will make their thinking visible to us, and especially to each other. Our intentional use of language can serve as a model for how people in school and in the world offer and seek inspiration, support, and kindness.

When we routinely use language like this:

- "Are you OK?"
- "Can you help me?"
- "Let's invite . . ."
- "This reminds me of you . . ."
- "Do you want to join us?"
- "Can I help?"

We hear children talking to each other like this:

- "Are you OK? I know you're sad because you forgot to bring your notebook from home, but you could share mine. I'll write on this side, and you can write on that side. We can write our names at the top so we can know whose are whose."

- "Can you help me figure this out? You know how you shared that trick your grandpa taught you about multiplication? The 'hand thing'? Can you show me that again? I keep forgetting the last part."

- "Let's invite Dionne to play with us during after-lunch recess today. He was all by himself yesterday—did you see him just sitting over there by the big tree?"

- "I found this awesome book called *The Proudest Blue*! There's a girl in it who reminds me of you! And her hijab is blue just like yours. Do you want to read it with me over by the window? I think you will really love it!"

- "Nora, do you want to join us? I know you're interested in mermaids—look at all the books we found in the library!"

- "Can I help you with that? I've had a lot of practice with getting zippers on coats unstuck."

When children speak to one another in these ways, they're showing us they understand that they're part of a community where everyone belongs—they're becoming aware and accepting of their needs and the needs of others, and they're developing a collection of strategies for what to say and do. They're learning what it's like and how it feels to be compassionate, caring, and kind. This too is where our power lives.

How Kids Sustain, Support, and Inspire Each Other

In communities where learners and learning thrive, children learn with and from each other. Sometimes this happens naturally, but it's too important to rely on serendipity alone. In Figure 3–5 you'll find examples of intentional, authentic routines that offer opportunities for kids (and their teachers) to sustain, support, and inspire each other throughout the school year.

How Kids Sustain, Support, and Inspire Each Other

The Action	Why It Matters	Give Me Some Specifics!
GETTING TO KNOW US!		
A short, topic-specific time for kids and their teachers to talk, share, listen and learn about each other. All year long!	This is about relationship building! It's hard to lift someone up, or accept a lift, when you don't know them very well! Outcomes? Kids and you: • talk about common interests • make new friends/deepen existing ones • have fun together • broaden understanding of others who are like/not like me • strengthen community ties—"We're the kinds of kids who . . ."	How long does it take? Five or so minutes once a week. When? Anytime! It could be during transition from one subject to another, first thing in the morning, before or after lunch, when kids need a short break . . . Who do kids partner with? Someone they haven't partnered with before! Then start over! Where do questions come from? Teachers and kids can ask: • "What are you reading?" • "Would you like to play the 'Would You Rather . . .?' game?" • "What are you writing about now?" • "When in the day do we need more choice?" • "What's your favorite thing to do at recess?" • "What's your favorite dessert or candy?" • "What's something you want to learn more about?" • "What's something you've learned how to do that you're proud of?"

Figure 3–5

The Action	Why It Matters	Give Me Some Specifics!
GALLERY WALKS/WALK-AROUNDS		
These "walks" get kids up and moving, learning from and with each other.	This is about kids learning from each other. These walks serve to: • open minds to new ideas and allow children to try something new • broaden perspectives and build appreciation for all the ways children figure things out • let children learn even more about each other. Kids think/say things like: • "I want to try that!" • "I never thought about doing it like that before . . ." • "That book looks so good. I'm going to ask _____ if I can borrow it when he's done." • "I want to learn more about this."	How long does it take? Five to ten minutes. When? During subject areas—reading, writing, math, social studies, art, choice learning. How does it work? Ask children who are willing to share to clear their desks and place on top: • their stack of books, or the book they're reading now • one way they've chosen to make their thinking visible • something they've made/ learned/done that they are proud of • how they solved a math problem • something they are working on and would like comments/feedback. (Sometimes Emily's kids bring sticky notes and/or clipboards to leave feedback and/or jot new ideas or things they want to try themselves.) (Everyone participates in the walk/kids decide if they want to share something.)

continues

The Action	Why It Matters	Give Me Some Specifics!
WALLS THAT SHOW WHO WE ARE AND HOW WE LEARN		
These kid-centered walls (and/or bulletin boards, doors, etc.) make learning and thinking visible, public. For examples, see pages 75 and 134–135.	Making children's thinking and learning public serves to: • honor/elevate children in their eyes and the eyes of others • inspire others to try something new • sustain and support one another.	Find wall space and post a range of ways kids show learner identity and agency within an invitation. These spaces are ongoing throughout the year—kids add as they continue to learn about themselves. These spaces include: • student work • kids' reflections • photos of kids at work/in process • kids' quotes.
REFLECTION AND SHARE CIRCLES		
Sometimes called a *debrief*, children come together to share, reflect, teach, and learn.		How long does it take? Ten to fifteen minutes. Usually at the end of a learning period, children gather (usually the whole group) to reflect on what they've learned about themselves that day. Children share reflections about: • what they tried, and how it went • what worked and what problems they had • what they learned about themselves (as a reader, writer, or mathematician) that they didn't know before • what's next for them • what surprised them. (Kids sometimes choose to bring clipboards, notebooks, and/or sticky notes to record things they want to try/think about/remember.)

We believe invitations offer children authentic opportunities for more togetherness—when we invite children to give something a try *and* reflect with one other about what they've learned about who they are and what they need as learners, they come to know each other in deeper, more wholehearted ways. Invitations go way beyond early in the year community-building activities. Invitations are all about kids doing the real work of learning and coming to honor and appreciate each other's histories, identities, talents, quirks, strengths, and struggles, all at the same time.

And we believe this too is true—the power and strength we feel when we're part of something bigger than ourselves doesn't leave us when the year ends or communities dissolve. Those experiences, that collective wisdom, energy, and strength, stay with us—that time, that place, and most of all those people, become part of who we are and how we view the world and our place in it.

Section 2

Into the Classroom!

You've read all about invitations—what they are, why they matter, possible questions to help you plan, and how they flourish in collaborative, caring communities. And now it's time to step into Emily's classroom and meet the children who bring them life, energy, and joy. We've included lots of photos in the section (Emily took them all in real time!) as well as a wide range of authentic, in-the-moment examples of kid work.

Each invitation will follow a predictable structure—below you'll find a "navigation guide" of our organizing features:

- **Getting started:** What might you need to know?

- **Planning:** What was our plan? How did we start?

- **Digging in:** What did we try? What happened? What did we learn?

- **Reflecting:** Where are we now?

Getting Started: What Might You Need to Know?

The first section includes information that's specific to each invitation:

- **Vision:** What's the best that could happen?

- **About this invitation:** What background knowledge might be helpful for you to know?

- **Research:** What research informs our practice and supports this invitation?

- **When will I launch it? When else can we practice?** After the invitation is launched, when else in the day might children practice and engage in this invitation?

  A star indicates when the invitations will be launched (in this case, reading), and the small blue circles show where else in the day kids could practice and engage in the invitation (in this case, writing, math, social studies, science, and choice time.)

- A note from Emily. This section will include personal reflections, past experiences, and notes to you.

Planning: What Was Our Plan?
How Did We Start?

This section includes:

- Emily's completed plan and the questions that guide her:

  1. Why does this invitation matter?

  2. What books, resources, and materials will children need?

  3. When will I launch it?

  4. What will I say?

  5. What reflective questions will I ask?

  6. How will I know what children need and how they are growing? How will I share with them what I've learned?

- A launching chart. This chart is created with children right after the invitation is opened and read—everyone is gathered together, talking and thinking about the invitation and what they might try. Emily facilitates the conversation and captures children's thinking.

- Examples of early kidwatching and subsequent planning notes. Even though Emily has a well-thought-out plan, she can't know exactly what children will do or what they'll need until they've had a chance to have a go. These early observations help her identify more clearly where kids actually are, allowing her to make adjustments to her original plan as needed.

A Note from Emily . . .

You might be a bit worried about this invitation. You might be wondering, "What if kids don't make the best choices? What if they choose books that are way too hard?" or maybe you're thinking, "There are so many foundational skills and comprehension strategies I need to teach them. They won't become great readers." It's OK to worry and wonder about these things. Here's the thing, all children won't make the best, "just-right" choices in the beginning. However, we won't know the kinds of choices they make until they have a chance to try. This is all about the process of giving children time to discover who they are as readers. And we'll be there to support them in their journey. Every week, they'll get a little bit better. We're there to watch them, listen to them, confer with them, and ask them questions.

To think about...
* Times/Experiences this week *
- Reading (by themselves and with partners)

☑ What if you could choose where to work?
★ Let's imagine...
- what spaces do we have?
- why might we go there?
- what spaces do we need?

Kid Watching → Choosing Spaces

* Kids are reflecting in different ways — pictures
— words
(in notebooks)

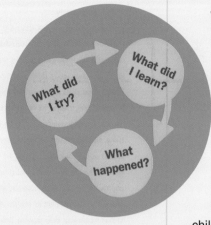

Digging In: What Did We Try? What Happened? What Did We Learn?

Once an invitation has been offered, you'll see how it unfolds over time. You may notice that the headings in this section are the same for each page: What did we try? What happened? What did we learn? That's because no matter where children are in the learning process (at the beginning, in the middle, or later), these reflective questions are a steadfast stick-together trio—thinking them through each step of the way is how children learn about themselves and develop a sense of agency.

We've also placed week 1, week 2, and week 3 alongside the headings to give you a general idea of how the invitation evolved, but there are no fixed timelines.

Reflecting: Where Are We Now?

This section shows where children are at this point of time, usually around three or four weeks into the invitation. But just because a chapter ends, it doesn't mean the invitation does! Though kids now know more about who they are and how they learn than they did before, they'll continue to apply and learn even more about each invitation and themselves in new settings and situations across the year.

And now, here we go! Find a comfy spot, grab a coffee or tea and a cookie or two, and meet Emily's kids. We're excited for you to spend some time thinking and learning with them, and we're pretty sure you're going to see your kids in hers. Happy reading!

what if you could choose where you want to work?

Why Would You go to the Bathtub?

- Partner reading
- to snuggle with Pillows and Stuffys
- laying at an angle
- if You wanted to Put Your feet out
- if You wanted to have somthing above Your head
- Dim light
- if You wanted books by you
- if you wanted to be a little off the ground
- get in the zone
- if You want People beside You
- if You wanted to read
- if you wanted people above You

Getting Started
What Might You Need to Know?

Vision

We envision children learning more about who they are and what they need when it comes to making choices about where to work: *What kind of learning/work am I going to be doing today? What kind of space will I need to do it?* We imagine kids asking themselves questions like these across subject areas, becoming more and more mindful about matching their learning purpose to where they need/choose to work.

About This Invitation

This invitation is all about children learning to make intentional decisions about where to work depending on their purpose. It begins with children having an understanding of how the room is organized. We ask them, "What kinds of spaces do you notice? What kinds of learning/work do you think you might do there?" Then it's about children digging in, trying out different spaces to discover for themselves what works and what doesn't. The key is for kids to spend a quiet moment thinking through their purpose *before* making their choices. Early on we might ask them, "What are you going to do in reading today? Now, imagine—where do you see yourself comfortably doing that? What kind of space will allow you to do what you need to do?" Then afterward (as always!), reflection—"How did the spot you chose work for you? What did you learn about yourself and what you need?"

This invitation can be introduced at any time, but it's particularly powerful when launched early in the year. Inviting children to make decisions about where they'll work based on their purpose sends an early message that you're not the kind of teacher who is going to be making all the decisions. Instead, you're the kind of teacher who trusts and believes in children,

what if you could choose where you want to work?

the kind of teacher who encourages everyone to learn to make important decisions for themselves and reflect on what happened and what they learned.

Research

When students practice how to make effective choices on a regular basis in school, they develop stronger decision-making skills. They grow in their ability to be self-reflective, thoughtful, and responsible people who can advocate for themselves and make appropriate decisions based on a wide variety of criteria (Anderson 2016).

When Will I Launch It? When Else Can We Practice?

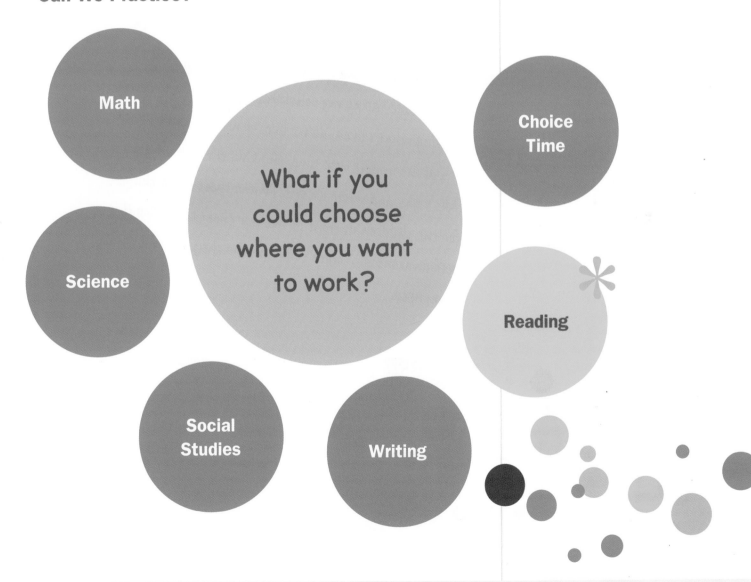

A Note from Emily . . .

We all work in different places and spaces for different reasons. I know that I'm the kind of person who likes to write in a comfy chair with my feet up, sit on the floor when I'm looking at kid work all spread out, or sit up front during a staff meeting (sometimes away from my friends so I don't get distracted). I know that when I'm reading, I need a quiet spot, and for planning, I need to be at a table facing my collaborators. And I wasn't born knowing what I liked, didn't like, or needed—I've learned this about myself over time, thinking through what feels right and what doesn't. I want these same things for the children in front of me—for them to develop this self-awareness in order to know who they are and what they need.

Planning
What Was Our Plan? How Did We Start?

Guiding Questions

1. Why might this invitation matter?

This invitation sets the tone from the very beginning—this year is going to be about kids learning to share in the responsibility for their learning in a variety of authentic ways throughout the day. Learning to link what you want/need to do with where you think you'll do it best is one of many ways children advance their identities as learners and develop a sense of agency.

2. What books, resources, and materials might children need?

Ensure there are a variety of defined spaces for individual kids, partnerships, and small groups to work comfortably.

3. When might I launch it?

X Reading _Writing __Math __Social Studies __Science __Choice Time
Or _

4. What might I say?

Now that we've opened the invitation, what are you thinking? Can you imagine choosing where you might need to work and learn?

Let's begin by taking a look around. What kinds of learning spaces do you see? If you want to, you can take a walk around the room. What learning spaces are you noticing? Why might you go there? Are there other spots we might need? (Listen in and record.) *When you choose a place to read today, think about what you're going to do as a reader and what kind of spot you'll need to do that. Talk with someone close to you about what you're thinking. . . .*

You have some good plans! But what if someone else is in the spot you're thinking about? What will you do? That's it—choose another spot! You might even discover something new about where you like to read and work.

After you read, we'll come back and share what you learned about yourselves as readers today, and *what you learned about the spaces you chose. I can't wait to find out what you learn! Off you go.*

5. What reflective questions might I ask?

- "Do you think about what you're going to do before you decide where you'll learn and work?"

- "How did your purpose affect your choice(s) today?"

- "What are you learning about yourself and what you need?"

6. How might I know what kids need and how they're growing? How might I share with them what I've learned?

- Kidwatch, listen in, study what kids make, confer

- Through personal notes to children; whole-group and small-group reflection circles; conferring; and short, in-the-moment conversations

Launching Chart

☑ **What if you could choose where you want to work?**

⭐ Let's imagine...
- <u>What</u> spaces do we have?
- <u>Why</u> might we go there?
- <u>What</u> spaces do we need?

- tables (Charlotte)
- rugs (JJ)
- coffee table (Atticus)
- chairs / couches (Anuli)
- bean bags (Serenity)
- bathtub (Vera)

- read
- make books
- work with a partner
- be in a group
- use math tools
- science experiments
- do research

✨ As you explore, think about...
- What am I going to do?
- Where might I go? Why?
- What am I learning about myself?

◀ After opening the invitation, Emily engages children in conversation by asking them to do some "imagining." Capturing children's thinking makes it visible and public: This is who we are and this is what we're digging into.

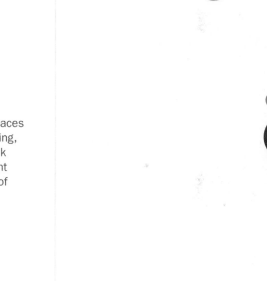

Planning Notes

To think about...

⭐ Times / Experiences this week ⭐

- Reading (by themselves and with partners)

- Math (exploration of tools - cubes and base 10 blocks)

- Writing (book making + sharing with others)

- Science (design challenges - partnerships and small groups)

⭐ ALWAYS going back to PURPOSE - What spaces are we choosing and why - WHAT are we learning about ourselves → Identity!!

◀ As kids explored spaces to work during reading, Emily begins to think about how this might look in other parts of the day.

Digging In: What Did We Try? What Happened? What Did We Learn? | WEEK 1

▼ From the very beginning, children reflect individually, with partners, and with the whole group about the kinds of spaces that worked for them, those that didn't, and why.

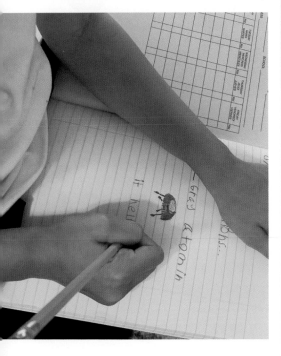

Kid Watching → Choosing Spaces

* Kids are reflecting in different ways — pictures — words (in notebooks)

♡ love how deliberate and earnest they are!!

* When they share with the whole class — there's a seriousness there → they're getting at identity and agency

↳ 'Who am I and what do I need as a learner' ♡

"I'm the Kind of Kid Who…"

> **rugs**
> Why: if you wanted to lay down
> Partner reading
> Why not: if you wanted to have
> your own space-if you wanted to
> sit up - comfy surface

▲ Demi and Anuli are deep in discussion, thinking through some of the purposes of different spaces. Why might they come to the rugs to work and learn? Why not?

Dear Demi and Anuli,
   I read your reflections about why you might go to the rugs. Wow! I noticed you're really thinking about why you would go there, but also why not. What other spaces are you going to try?
   ♡ Love,
      Mrs. Callahan

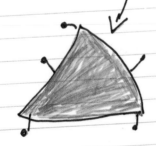

I sat at a triangle ottomen...

At first I sat at my table and it didn't work for me because there was too many people around me. I thought that it would be a great spot but it turned out it wasn't.

I prefer reading spred apart.

◄ Aiden showed how his thinking changed in his reflection: "At first I thought, but it turned out . . ." This shows his understanding of the process of reflection: *What did I try? What happened? What did I learn about myself?* It's this process that will continue to help him learn more about who he is as a learner and what he needs.

"I'm the Kind of Kid Who..."

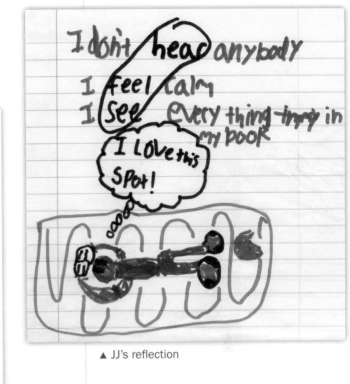

Day 1 |Reading Reflections|

I liked the Blue couch Because there was Lots of space at first I thot I was going to like the Gray ottoman But it just was not right.

Day 2
Laying Down helped me But Being Next to my friend Distracted me from reading.

▲ Caleb's reflections

▲ JJ's reflection

now I like the corner in the book Shelfs because I like the Darkness because I don't like light in my eyes.

▲ Caitlin's reflection

As children try out different spaces, Emily kidwatches and makes notes about their choices, to learn more about them. Sometimes she takes photos, prints them, and invites kids to paste them in their notebooks if they'd like. Having access to the actual photo helps kids anchor/remember their experiences and can deepen their reflections.

▲ Kendell reflects in his notebook.

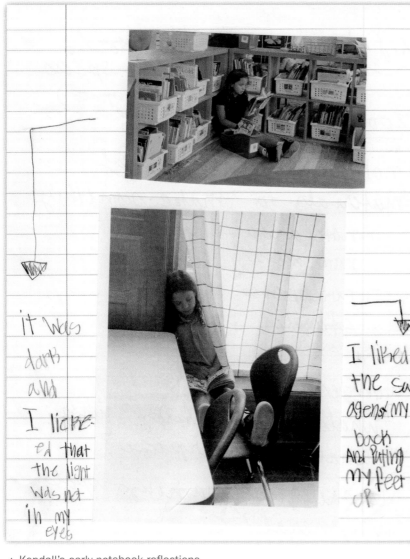

it was
dark
and
I licked
ed that
the light
was not
in my
eyes

I liked
the sun
agenst my
back
And Puting
my feet
up

▲ Kendall's early notebook reflections

Dear Kendall,
    I noticed that you're
reflecting on why these
spots worked for you
in reading. This has
me wondering — what
works for you when
you're doing other
things — like math
or making books?
I can't wait to talk
and learn more!
        ♡ Love,
          Mrs. Callahan

▲ Emily nudges Kendall to
consider/reflect on her
choices in other subject
areas too.

Kid Watching → Choosing /
Exploring Spaces
(reflecting on spots)

Zooey

* noticings — using lots of
materials to 'make something'
      - notecards
      - markers
      - notebooks
      - stapler

* wonderings—
    - what's she making? why?
    ↳ What's her purpose?

    - is she just naming spots
    in general?

    - Are they about which
    ones work for her?

* meet to confer with her!
                    ☺

▲ When we kidwatch, we don't always know for sure what's going on. Emily jots notes about what "might be," and she will follow up with Zooey in a conference to learn more. What did she find out? Well . . . Zooey was "naming all the places I could work" on note cards, and then, depending on her purpose, "I'll try one out and write on the card what happened!"

If the Donut is full I can go to the couch, carpet, pillow, ottoman, wait for the Bathtub, Loft — you should not rush — wait till everybody gets a turn. Wait till tomorrow or a week.

▲ JJ loves to read while sitting on the "donut." But if someone else is already there, no worries! There are plenty of other places to go. (And a little "self-talk" is always helpful!)

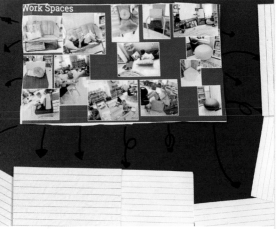

Kid Watching — Collaborating
to share what
♡ were learning
about ourselves
and each other

✳ Now kids are going beyond
themselves and what they
need - because they are
talking, sharing, reflecting,
questioning each other →
- they are learning
MORE about EACH OTHER
and what they need
as learners too!

✳ need to reflect whole
group about all the
things we've learned ♡♡

◄ Serenity and Zooey chose to glue
some of the printed photographs
onto chart paper. "Let's see if we
can learn about what everyone
needs." (Learning about what
others need leads to acceptance,
appreciation, and tolerance.)

▲ JJ makes his learning about Gavin visible!

Dear Gavin and JJ,
I was listening in on
your conversation and
heard you talking about
going somewhere
different if your
favorite place is taken.
I'm wondering—how are you
making these decisions?
And when you're ready,
could you share your
reflection with the
class? Just let me
know! ☺   Love,
                ♡ Mrs. Callahan

Gavin Likes the
Library area... if the
Library area is not open
He will find another
        space! (a space that
              will fit him—
                    he needs
                    Quiet too!)

Reflecting: Where Are We Now?

▶ Near the end of the first month of school, Emily and her kids learned a new child would soon be joining their classroom community. Eager to help them feel comfortable and welcome, a group of children decided to make a book to show them all the learning spaces they could choose from, complete with an individual tour during choice time! See the following pages for the rest of their book.

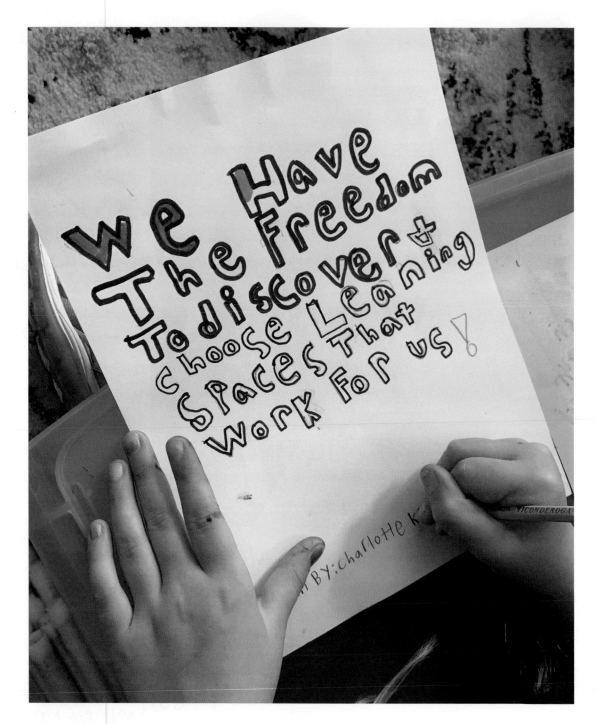

Why might you choose
the tables

You could...

do Solo Work

do Partner Work

use the I Pads

eat Lunch

go to calm down

Color With markers

These Spaces are
Versatile!

alwase available

different Sizes

How many
ofen?

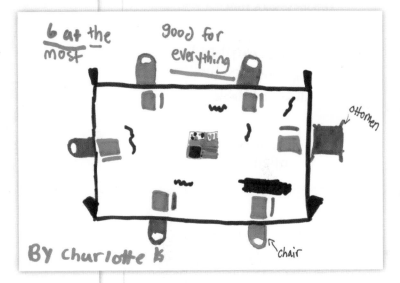

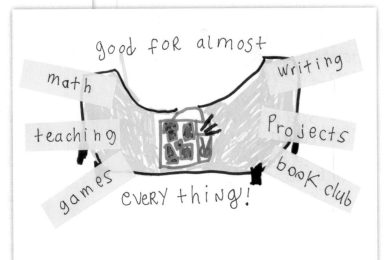

▲ Tables with notes about what they might
do there

Why might you choose the
open areas?

you could do...
    Solo Work
    Partner Work
    IPad Work
    big Projects
    lessons-Work time-Share

These Spaces are
    good for everything!
    the most versatile
    alwase available

    How many
    open ?

Dear Vera, Ryker, Zoey,
Charlotte, and Scarlett,
    I read your final
version of your 'spaces
book' and I just wanted
to say thank you! I
noticed you really
thought about all of
the spaces in our
classroom (we really do
have so many places to
work don't we?!).
    This will be so
helpful for not only
our new student, but
also for all of us as
reminders if we need
it!
        Love,
        Mrs. Callahan

▲ Emily's note to the authors

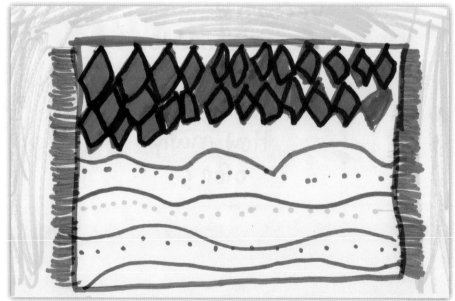

▲ Rug in open area

Why might you choose
the Loft?

you could do ...

    Partner work

    Solo work
    Write if you are
    really motivated

This Space...

    IS comfortable
    has Pillows
    gives you a birds eye View!

      How many?
      1-3

Why might you choose
the couches

you could do...
    Solo Work
    Work on IPads (zearn, EPic)
    Partner Work

This Space helps you...
    Sit up Straight
    Keep awake
    get your work done

It is
    Comfortable but not too Comfortuble
    By Lots of books

      How many?
      Grey 1-2
      Blue 2-4

As children developed deeper awareness and understanding of who they are and what they need as learners, they began to think about their spaces at home, too! Check out what their spots looked like outside school.

I think my favorite spot is the couch. It's warm and there is a lot of pillows. I like when I use my blanket and the light is off because the sun is out. We open the blinds for natural sunlight.

▲ JJ's thinking about different spaces he has to read at home

Sometimes at the table I read and thats okay. The sunlight is nice and if I have a snack after breakfast to go with it.
It's a long table and I sit in my seat with my blanket and read my book.

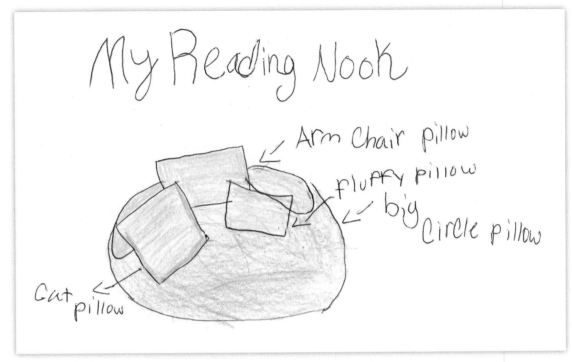

▲ Charlotte's sketch

▲ Isaiah's reflection

What if you could choose your own materials?

Getting Started
What Might You Need to Know?

Vision

We envision children developing an ongoing awareness of the materials available to them and understanding what, why, and how they might use them. Over time, we imagine their inner conversations sounding something like this: "I want to show what I know about the life cycle of a frog, so I'm going to need a big piece of paper, some colored pencils to draw and color with, and a thin, dark-colored marker to outline and label each part of the cycle. And I'm going to need a big space to work." Or "We want to keep track of our questions as we read, so we're going to need two colors of sticky notes—one color for our questions, and another color when we figure out some answers. And we're going to make a little book so we can keep all of our thinking together."

what if you could
choose your
own materials?

About This Invitation

This invitation is about children becoming aware of the materials that are available to them and learning to use them in purposeful ways. In the beginning, it's all about exploration—*What do I want to do or make? What materials might I need to do that? What do I want to try?* And it's also about reflection—*How did my choice(s) work out? Depending on what I want to do, what might I try next?*

These early reflections and conversations, just as in all invitations, send a clear and consistent message that you believe they're the kind of kids who can figure things out.

Some children may initially ask you questions like the following ones—as though they just can't quite believe they have the power to make their own decisions!

- "So how many markers can we have?" ("How many do you think you'll need? You can always put away extras or come back for more.")

- "What kind of paper can we use?" ("Any kind! Think about your purpose—what kind and size do you think you'll need? Then, make a choice, try it out, and see what happens.")

- "Can I use the stapler?" ("Of course you can! You remember where they are, right? And next time, you don't even need to ask.")

Some children may already have a sense about what they need and why, but we want to broaden their perspectives too, encouraging everyone to explore using materials in new, purposeful, and creative ways.

And remember, this invitation isn't just about choosing materials—it's about kids coming to understand more about who they are and about what they need, creating early pathways to identity and agency.

Throughout this invitation in Emily's class, you'll notice children trying out materials mostly in response to their reading—in later invitations you'll see how this early work supports kids when making their thinking visible in deeper, more complex ways in reading and across the day. But it's this early work (exploration and reflection) that allows them to use the materials with purpose and ease later.

You might want to think throughout these beginning weeks about opportunities for children to explore different materials. During various class times, you might ask them the following questions:

- **Reading/read-alouds:** "What do you want to remember forever? What materials might you use to show that?"

- **Writing/bookmaking:** "What kind of book do you want to make? What kind of paper do you imagine you'll need? What other materials might you want to use?"

- **Math:** "What might you use to make your thinking strategies visible?"

- **Science:** "What might you use to show your learning from this design challenge?"

Before launching this invitation, think about providing as many possibilities for choice as you can—pencils, different kinds of markers, crayons, different sizes and types of paper (lined and unlined), varied sizes and colors of sticky notes if you use them, scissors, staplers and staples, and clay, and anything else you can get your hands on! The more choices you are able to offer children, the more opportunities they'll have to learn and grow.

Next, think about how you will organize materials for easy access—buckets or baskets? Shelves? Storage bins? Kids can help by sorting, placing, and creating labels. Emily sometimes uses "exploration boxes" so kids can have a little "kit" of all the available writing materials and sticky notes to try. They refine their boxes as they learn more about what works best for them, asking themselves: *What's my purpose? What will I need? What will I try?*

Research

As Anne Haas Dyson (1993) said, "A child must have some version of, 'Yes, I imagine I can do this.' And the teacher must also view the present child as competent, and on that basis, imagine new possibilities."

When Will I Launch It? When Else Can We Practice?

Math

Reading

Science

What if you could choose your own materials?

Choice Time

Social Studies

Writing

A Note from Emily . . .

My mom told me some of her favorite memories of when I was little was when she'd let me pick out a new box of crayons. I can vividly remember opening up a new box, smelling them, and saying "Awwww, there's nothing like a new box of crayons smell." I lived for trips to the craft store to pick out new markers, pencils, and different kinds of notebooks.

And now, thirty-plus years later, I'm still the kind of person who loves all kinds of materials. I use this kind of notebook and this pencil when I'm taking notes when conferring with children. I use this kind of paper when I'm mapping out my thinking for a new unit of study and these kinds of markers when making charts. I use big sticky notes for making my thinking visible when reading informational text and smaller ones when adding on to my thinking in my notebook. All of these intentional choices I make for myself are the same intentional choices I want for the children in front of me. I want to give them time and space to make decisions, try new things, explore, and reflect—to learn about who they are, what they need, and why they need it. And I want all of this to happen on purpose at school (not just at home like I experienced).

What If You Could Choose Your Own Materials?

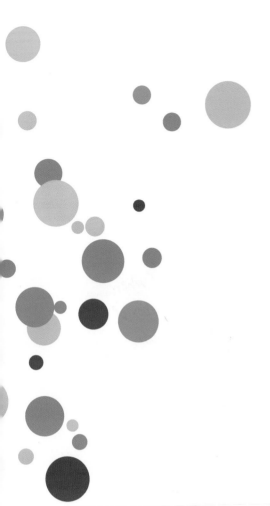

Planning
What Was Our Plan? How Did We Start?

Guiding Questions

1. Why might this invitation matter?

When we offer children opportunities to choose their own materials, they learn to make thoughtful choices: What do I want to do? What materials might I need to do it? Making their own decisions personalizes their work, giving it distinction, character, and depth.

2. What books, resources, and materials might children need?

Materials: Make sure bins are well stocked and organized with markers, pencils, pens, staplers and staples, varieties of paper, minibooks, sticky notes, paper clips, index cards, and so on.

3. When might I launch it?

_X_ Reading __Writing __Math __Social Studies __Science
__Choice Time Or __

4. What might I say?

Morning Everyone! This invitation is all about learning more about all the materials we have and how you might use them to show your thinking and learning. It's about knowing your purpose—What thinking and learning do I want to show? What materials will I need to do it?

First, let's think of all the materials we have and make a list. (Record responses on launching chart.) *Now let's think about how and why we might use them . . . When and why might you use a pencil? Markers? Sticky notes or a big piece of paper?*

Take a look at some of the things I do . . . I use sticky notes and a pencil when I want to jot down something quickly . . . see this one where I have a question? And here I've used unlined paper and thin markers to help me understand and remember what's important. And look at this entry in my notebook—What do you notice about this page?

This week you'll be exploring different materials to make your thinking and learning visible—What's my purpose? (What do I want to do?) How will I do it? (What materials will I need?)

Let's start with our read-aloud from this morning—What from the story is going to stick with you? What do you want to remember? Once you have some ideas, think about what materials you want to try in order to show your thinking. It's going to be fun to find out what you tried and what you're learning about yourselves!

5. What reflective questions might I ask?

- "What are you learning about how you use markers (or sticky notes, minibooks, other kinds of paper . . .)?"

- "How does thinking about what you want to do help guide you in choosing your materials?"

- "I'm the kind of kid who uses _____ when I want to
_____."

6. How might I know what kids need and how they're growing? How might I share with them what I've learned?

- Kidwatch, listen in, study what kids make, confer

- Through personal notes to children; whole-group and small-group reflection circles; conferring; and short, in-the-moment conversations

Launching Chart

What if you could choose your own materials?

★ Let's imagine...
- <u>What</u> materials do we have?
- <u>Why</u> might we use them?

· pencils
· pens
· markers
· sticky-notes
· paper
· mini-books
· notebooks

★ As you explore and try these out, think about...
- What am I going to do?
- What do I need to do it?
- What am I learning about myself?

Planning Notes

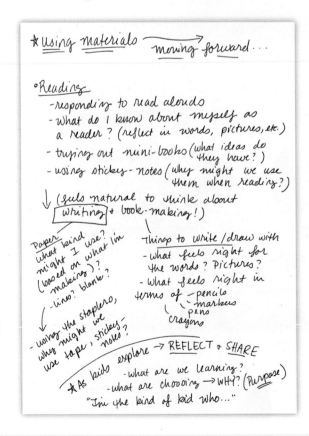

★ Using materials → moving forward...

° Reading
- responding to read alouds
- what do I know about myself as a reader? (reflect in words, pictures, etc.)
- trying out mini-books (what ideas do they have?)
- using sticky-notes (why might we use them when reading?)

↓ (feels natural to think about [writing] + book-making!)

Paper
what kind might I use? (based on what I'm making?) - lines? blank?

- using the staplers, why might we use tape, stickies, notes?

- Things to write/draw with
- what feels right for the words? Pictures?
- what feels right in terms of - pencils, markers, pens, crayons

★ As kids explore → REFLECT & SHARE
- what are we learning?
- what are choosing → WHY? (Purpose)
"I'm the kind of kid who..."

◄ Once kids are out and about, Emily takes time to do some kidwatching and listening in. She already has a well-thought-out plan, but she can't really know what will happen until kids are in the midst of "doing." Noticing and recording what she sees and hears helps her imagine new possibilities for children to choose materials in other subject areas throughout the day.

Digging In: What Did We Try? What Happened? What Did We Learn? | WEEK 1

Everyone shared what they tried, what happened, and what they learned during reflection and share time.

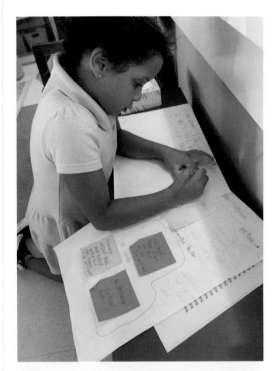

▲ Theo tried out the stapler to attach a drawing to his writing. "It's faster than glue."

Kendall tried out a big piece of paper, sticky notes, and a pencil to keep track of her questions in reading, and later in the day she decided to try out a legal pad to make a list of story ideas in writing.

▲ Kahlil and Kash kept track of books they wanted to read. Kahlil tried out a minibook, and Kash decided he was a list-making kind of kid and chose a sticky note and pen. "We are doing the same thing in different ways!"

▲ Jericho tried out sticky notes, markers, pens, and a half sheet of paper to respond to *I Am Every Good Thing* by Derrick Barnes. "I used markers and pens to draw my picture and then I wrote my words on the sticky note to put on top."

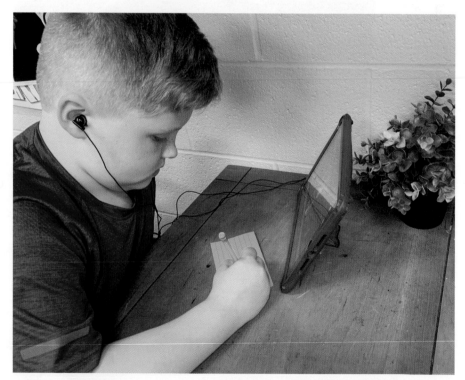

▲ As he listened to an audio book, Chase tried out sticky notes to sketch his learning. "Next time I'm going to try a bigger sticky note with no lines so I can fit in my drawing better."

▲ Kaybrie tried stapling half sheets of paper for her new book. "I used pens and colored pencils for my pictures and this cool marker to make certain words stand out."

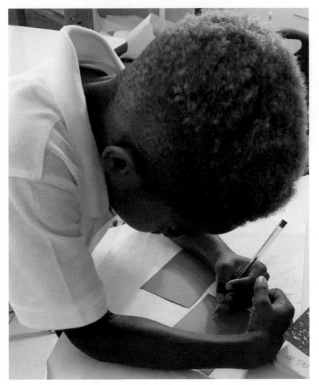

◀ Demi tried out dry erase markers on the table to share the big ideas in a story she'd just read. "When I get it how I want it, I'm going to write it on a big piece of paper so I can share it."

▲ Gavin tried out sticky notes to show his different strategies in math. "I used different-colored pens for my different strategies."

I AM the KiND OF KiD
WHO NeeDS gel PeNS
SO I CAN COleR CODE
—EliZA

I like STiCKY notes.
because you can change
your mind. you can Just
change your mind. and
Take Them off if you want
To.

▲ The girls' reflections

▲ These two think big pieces of paper, sticky notes, and gel pens are just what they need to do their best thinking work!

◄ Emily placed these guiding questions close to the materials to serve as gentle reminders. She also created space for children to share what they've tried to honor their efforts *and* to support, inspire, and sustain others.

▲ Emily noticed Kaybrie using the to-go basket to "shop" for markers and decided to confer with her to learn more about her choices.

✱ Kids are exploring/using materials ✱ !!! ☺

(starting to 'shop' for certain things, putting things back, etc.)

↓

✱ Noticing — Kaybrie (using basket)
- seems really thoughtful and careful when choosing →
- what's she choosing? why? (purpose)

↓ ✱ Conference

Me- You have lots in your basket! when you look at your choices — what are you learning about yourself? (has LOTS of colors ☺)
(Prompting — 'I'm the kind of kid who...')

Kaybrie - '...loves colors - I think it's because I love art filled with colors... and if I mess up with a sharpie - like if I get out of line or something - I can attach it to something else and make something new with my mind"

✱✱✱ (Me) → she knows she's the kind of kid who sees mistakes as opportunities to create something new!!!. ♡♡♡

▲ Wait! Minibooks in math? You bet! Caleb thought it would be a perfect way to keep track of the strategies he was learning. "Every time I learn a new strategy, I'm going to write it on a new page to help me remember it!"

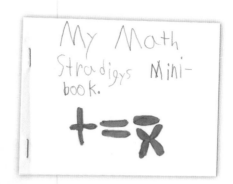

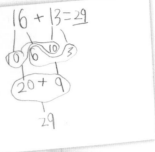

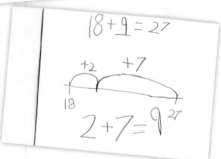

Even though We are diffirint...We can still work together.

♡

~Lilah.

this book is to teach you that you can't always be inside watching TV and looking at screens all day! Maybe you Should get outside with friends and family for Playing and getting fresh air!

◀ After Emily read aloud *Strictly No Elephants* by Lisa Mantchev, Lilah jumped up and headed for the big sticky notes. "I just have to write my thinking on a big sticky note so I can share it with everybody!" Wyatt thought this was a good idea too. Here's his big idea from *The Couch Potato* by Jory John.

I am The kind of kid who heeds a LOT of space To show my Thinking and draw.

markers | Pencils | pens | Sharpies

I'm the kind of kid who Likes marker

▲ Atticus is curious. "How do I know what works best for me?" He decided to get a red "to-go basket," select different writing materials, and "do some research about what I use for different things."

◀ Emily's always saying to children, "Put your thinking on the page in whatever way makes sense to you." And they do. During their first writing unit ("We Are Authors and We Make Books") McKayla designed her own story structure, and later, when she decided she wanted to write poems, she knew she needed something different. Yes, it's an organizer. But it's *her* organizer!

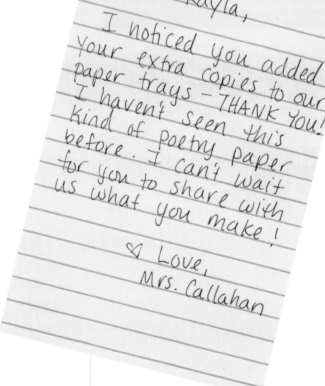

Dear McKayla,

I noticed you added your extra copies to our paper trays — THANK YOU! I haven't seen this kind of poetry paper before. I can't wait for you to share with us what you make!

♡ Love,
Mrs. Callahan

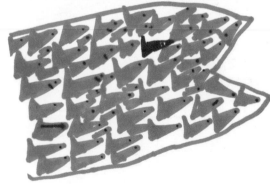

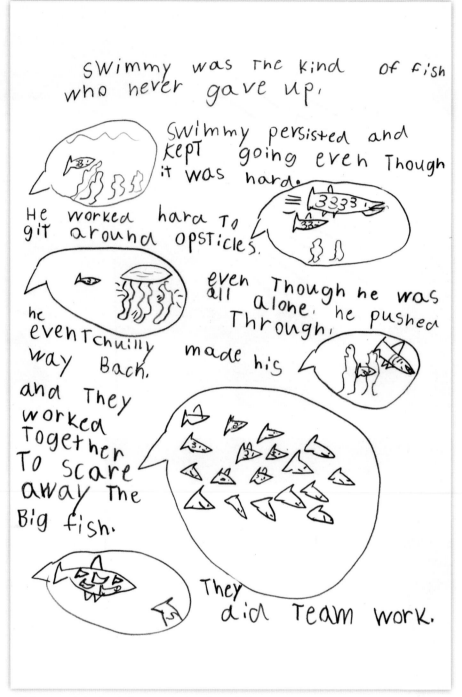

▲ Talen loved the book *Swimmy* by Leo Lionni. He read it again and again and finally decided he wanted to "honor Swimmy" by sharing everything that little black fish had taught him. And he decided a "giant piece of chart paper" was just what he needed.

▼ Anuli and Bella were fans of pencils and pens. But they wondered, "How can we explain to everyone the difference?" They decided to create a table in their notebooks, "just in case someone might want some ideas."

Dear Bella and Anuli,
    Wow! You really thought about lots of different reasons to use pens vs. pencils! I'm wondering, how do you decide which "parts that are special" when using a pen? I can't wait to learn more when we meet!
                    ♡ Love,
                    Mrs. Callahan

When to use a Pencil!	When to use a Pen!
Drafting	Publishing
Writing Somthig Short	Projects
Test	Self grading
Post its	Highlighting
Focusing Matters	a part thats Speshal
When you don't know how to spell a word	Writers block
	book resonse
	pen pencil

This thinking prompted more discussion about other materials—why use markers? Yes, markers are fun and colorful, but what's their purpose? When and why might you need color? Why red versus blue, thin tip versus fine tip? And when do you just need to use a pencil?

I like writing my thinken or sticky notes and putting it altogether. It's kind of like a painting at a art fair... you have to put all the detalis together to see it

I am the kind of kid who Has tons of words that I can write them down and orginize it in my notebook or on Postit notes in a way that makes sense to me — Charlotte K

Making my own orginization system makes sense to me so that I can understand and so that others can understand too.

▲ Written reflections, and the illustrations that accompany them, help children think more deeply about their choices. You'll notice a more sophisticated awareness of who they are and what they need and the ability to articulate it in ways they weren't able to do before.

Asking children to reflect on what they're learning sends the message that their work matters and promotes their senses of identity and agency. "I'm the kind of kid who…"

Henry and Zoeyayn noticed a problem: "Not that many kids are using sticky notes, and we don't understand why." They decided to interview other kids who used them too (below) and then set out to think more about how and why they use sticky notes so they might inspire others to give them a try!

Video 5–1 » Listen to Henry and Zoeyayn figuring out all the different purposes of sticky notes.

See page ix to access the online video.

I use sticky-notes for...
1. holding on to my thinking in books
2. sketching idea's in writing
3. jotting in sience
4. Doing math sometimes

▲ Zoeyayn and Henry work to figure out how the sizes of sticky notes serve different purposes.

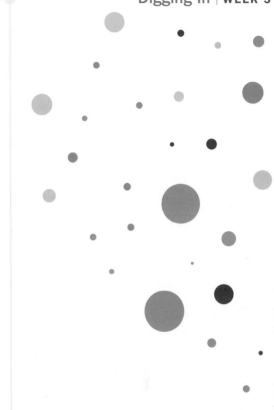

Why Might You use small Post-it's?

↗Like this ♡ ? ! ?!

You could use Little symbols
also you could use
small Post-its for
Jotting Down small
thingking

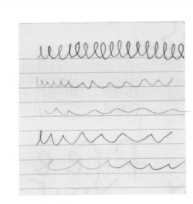

Why might you use Lines?

Neat Handrighting

Adding on to thinking

Organize your thinking

meideim Post-it
↓
want to tell a friend but its not the Best time! or Jotting Down short thingking or Reminders!

Big Post-it
↓
big thingking or growing on to other\Dif thinoking

Large post-it(poster)
↓
teaching or showing thinking behind your teaching

▲ Zoeyayn and Henry think deeper about why and how they might use certain sticky notes.

Dear Henry and Zoeyayn,
I wanted to say thank you for doing some research and helping us think about so many ways to use sticky notes! I've never thought about using different colors for different emotions— I'm excited to try this out myself!
Where do you think you'll display your charts for everyone to see?
♡ Love,
Mrs. Callahan

P.S. I really like large, lined sticky notes! ☺

Mini Poster

Large

mini rage

medium lines

medium

Regular

Small mini

Sizes

Color Coding

Emotions

Red / Pink   Yellow   orange   green   blue

mad   Happy   confused   Discusted   Sad

Diffrent colors could mean emotions

sections

orange = koalas   Yellow = girrafes   green = Plants   blue = water   pink = famigos

feel free to try your own

▲ Color-coding charts, sections, and examples of the sizes, colors, and kinds of sticky notes children can access. (We love how they used the phrases "could mean" and "feel free to try your own." They know it's all about choice and options!) Thanks for all the new ideas, Henry and Zoeyayn!

Reflecting: Where Are We Now?

My Favorites Box!
☆ markers to color with! To draw pictures!
☆ Sharpies to draw outlines! like smiles and eyes!
☆ favorite pens to use for little details.
☆☆ special big pen that clicks for different colors.

Stress box!
★ I have sticky notes to write down my sad thoughts to get them out of my head.
☆ I have tissues if I need to wipe of my tears.
★ I have a old eraser I color on sometimes too.

▲ Meet Lilah! After she'd created her very own Favorites Box, she decided she needed a Stress Box, too. "Sometimes I get worried or sad and have big feelings about things. So I made a little box of stuff to help me when I need it—like if I get sad or something, I can just go to my Stress Box so I can calm down and be all ready to learn."

Getting Started
What Might You Need to Know?

Vision

We imagine a daily, thirty minutes (at least!) free-choice independent reading time where children are happily reading, writing, thinking, and talking about books and ideas, all the while discovering more about themselves and each other as readers. We picture a lively and joyful reading culture that promises authenticity and promotes a deep love of reading.

About This Invitation

This invitation is about encouraging and inspiring children to find out more (and to be curious about) who they are as readers: *Who am I as a reader now? What kind of reader am I becoming? What kind of reader do I want to be?* Sometimes we focus so much of our attention on the processes of reading that we forget the bigger picture. This invitation encourages kids to explore a more expansive definition of reading, exploring and experiencing what readers do in the world.

At the beginning of the year, we invite children to explore book tubs and the classroom library, talk about books, and learn a variety of strategies for how to choose books they can and want to read. In the weeks to come, they'll learn more about making their thinking visible, recommending books to each other and taking part in spontaneous book clubs if they so choose.

It's up to you where you place independent reading time. Emily places it within her literacy block, but it could also be a separate, stand-alone time at the beginning of the day, at the end, or somewhere in between. The important thing is that kids have time every day to choose books and reading materials they're interested in and want to read.

Emily strives to create a culture of readers and reading, where children have daily opportunities to discover even more about themselves and each other by engaging in the kinds of things readers do the world over:

What if you could choose to learn more about yourself as a reader?

What if you could choose to do what readers do in the world?

- Readers explore books.

- Readers choose books they can and want to read.

- Readers talk about books.

- Readers choose how they'll make their thinking and learning visible.

- Readers recommend books to one another.

- Readers take part in book clubs.

Independent reading doesn't mean children read in isolation! It's a wondrous time where everyone chooses what and where they want to read and if they'll read on their own, with a partner, or in a small group. In other words, it's all about choice and reading love.

This daily independent reading time is in addition to the explicit teaching of reading processes, where children learn about surface structures, including decoding and fluency, and deeper structures, including vocabulary and strategies for comprehension.

Research

Providing students with choices about what to read, where to read, and with whom produced an impact on reading achievement more than three times as large as reported for systematic phonics instruction alone (Guthrie and Humenick 2004).

When Will I Launch It? When Else Can We Practice?

Math
Who am I as a mathematician?

Choice Time
Who am I as an artist and creator?

What if you could choose to learn more about yourself as a reader? What if you could choose to do what readers do in the world?

Science
Who am I as a scientist?

Reading
Who am I as a reader?

Social Studies
Who am I as a historian?

Writing
Who am I as a writer?

On the next few pages you'll read about "exploration tubs," where we collect a selection of books for kids to explore early in the year to find out more about themselves as readers: *What kinds of books am I most interested in? Which ones draw me in? Which ones make me happy?* We're not concerned about readability right now—this is simply about kids finding out more about the kinds of books they like/ are intrigued by most at this point in time.

These two pages will give you some background information about the exploration tubs themselves. What's in them? What do we consider when creating them? What's the bigger picture? The books we place in these tubs are intentional—we're not about just filling them up with a bunch of books! We're striving to be inclusive and to ensure that all kids have access to a wide range of topics, levels, and themes and that there are enough books available that can act as both "mirrors, windows, and sliding glass doors" for all our children (Bishop 1990).

Examples of the kinds of books included in exploration tubs include:

- Fiction, like *The Proudest Blue, All Are Welcome,* and *Carmela Full of Wishes*
- Nonfiction, like *Actual Size, Who Would Win?* and *One Tiny Turtle*
- Poetry, like *Can I Touch Your Hair? Forest Has a Song,* and *Change Sings*
- Wordless books, like *A Circle of Friends, Another,* and *The Farmer and the Clown*
- Graphic novels, like *Dog Man, Stunt Boy, in the Meantime,* and The Baby-Sitters Club series
- Early readers like Elephant and Piggie, Max and Zoe, and Fly Guy
- Books that have been read aloud, like *The Day You Begin, The Water Protectors, Lubna and Pebble,* and *Eyes that Kiss at the Corners*

A Note from Emily . . .

You might be a bit worried about this invitation. You might be wondering, "What if kids don't make the best choices? What if they choose books that are way too hard?" Or maybe you're thinking, "There are so many foundational skills and comprehension strategies I need to teach them. They won't become great readers." It's OK to worry and wonder about these things. Here's the thing, all children won't make the best, "just-right" choices in the beginning. However, we won't know the kinds of choices they make until they have a chance to try. This is all about the process of giving children time to discover who they are as readers. And we'll be there to support them in their journey. Every week, they'll get a little bit better. We're there to watch them, listen to them, confer with them, and ask them questions.

Planning
What Was Our Plan? How Did We Start?

Guiding Questions

1. Why might this invitation matter?

Through exploration and discovery, this invitation encourages children to learn more about what readers do in the world, helping them gain a deeper understanding of what reading is, what readers do, and who they are as readers.

2. What books, resources, and materials might children need?

Prepare book tubs for each table—include a variety of fiction, nonfiction, poetry, wordless, early readers, and so on, and ensure all children are represented in each set of books.

3. When might I launch it?

_X_ Reading _Writing __Math __Social Studies __Science ___Choice Time
Or __

4. What might I say?

Good morning, everyone! This invitation is all about discovering more about yourselves and each other as readers. I know you already know a lot. You're learning about the strategies you use to figure out words and make meaning as you read, you know the kinds of spaces that work best for you, and lots of other things, too.

This invitation is about doing the kinds of things readers do in the world. Let's think about that for a minute—can you think of someone you know who loves to read? Can you picture them in your mind? What do they do? (Record what they say, and transfer to a chart after school.)

You know how I sometimes ask you to choose a specific type of text depending on our units? Like for a nonfiction study you need to choose nonfiction books, or if it's a poetry unit, you'll need poetry books?

But during this independent reading time, there are no limits on the type of genre you'll choose from—that's up to you! You can choose any book you can and want to read.

Let's begin by exploring the books we have in our classroom. See all the tubs on the tables? You'll have a chance to explore them all this week. This is one way to get to know more about yourself as a reader—what books are you most interested in?

I can't wait to see what you discover about yourselves during share and reflection time.

5. What reflective questions might I ask? (now and throughout the year) increasing levels of sophistication

- "What new things are you learning about yourself as a reader?"

- "What kinds of books interest you most?"

- "How are you growing as a reader?"

- "Is there a book that has changed the way you see the world?"

- "Is there a book that has shaped who you are? A character who has inspired you?"

- "What book or books do you think you'll remember forever? Why?"

6. How might I know what kids need and how they're growing? How might I share with them what I've learned?

- Kidwatch, listen in, study what kids make, confer

- Through personal notes to children; whole-group and small-group reflection circles; conferring; and short, in-the-moment conversations

Launching Chart

What if you could choose to learn more about yourself as a reader?

⭐ Let's imagine...
What do readers do? **READ!**

- read all kinds of books
- go to the library
- my mom reads on her iPad
- sound out words
- my grandma keeps a book in her car
- share books with friends
- learn new stuff from nonfiction
- read magazines
- talk about books
- read stuff online
- listen to books

- go to the book store
- order books online
- find comfy spots
- read before bed

⭐ As you explore, think about...
- What are you doing as a reader in our room?
- What kinds of books are you exploring?
- What kinds of books do you like?
- What are you learning about yourself as a reader?

◄ Chart created with children during the launch: Let's imagine: What do readers do in the world?

Planning Notes

✱ Exploring Books → Moving Forward, to think about...

→ Tubs at tables
- Variety of books in tubs —
  → ✱ Poetry & Song books — various authors — not all rhyming
  ✱ Picture books
  - all children represented
  - Stories of different experiences
  - mix of genres
  ✱ Informational books
    - all about books
    - variety of topics
    - true stories - diverse cultures

→ Logistics
- rotate tubs each day — over course of the week — want kids exposed to all
- choice in where to explore - at tables, finding a spot, explore with friends
- put books back in correct tubs

✱ Always Reflecting & Sharing → Guiding !!!
                                Questions ...

◄ Emily thinks through logistics.

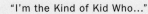

Digging In: What Did We Try? What Happened? What Did We Learn? | WEEK 1

Readers Explore Books

Imagine browsing your way through books at your local library or bookstore with a friend. You've given yourselves the gift of time to skim the pages, looking for something to read that's interesting and new. You quietly chat about books, authors, and more, and the chances are good you leave with at least one or two books you can't wait to read. Emily works to create these same opportunities in the classroom. Early in the year, children learn about books that are in their classroom (and school) library through exploration—they, too, browse their way through books placed in book tubs at their tables. She creates five exploration tubs and rotates them each day for five days. Kids skim the pages, read, and reflect on their own and with each other about the books that interest them most, and return them to their tables at the end of independent reading. And throughout the rest of the week, they'll have brand-new tubs of books to explore!

▲ (bottom) "There is so much to think about in graphic novels!"

◄ When asked after a read-aloud, "Who wants to do some more thinking about *Mr. Tiger Goes Wild?*" Gavin couldn't wait to dig in!

What books are we interested in?

Jericho - Froggy, Pete the Cat
Jaycee - Animal books
Kahlil - Fly Guy Presents Bats
Kash - The Magic Fish
Chase - Dog Man
Lilah - Elephant and Piggie
Seth - Who Would Win
Taylin - Elephant and Piggie
Karmiin - Wolfie the Bunny
Demi - Max and Zoe
Gavin - Volcanoes
Reiley - Wordless Books
Elijah - Sharks!

Bella - Layla's Happiness
Micha - Splat the Cat
Huxley - Read! Read! Read!
Isaiah - Guinness Book of World Records
Scarlett - Narwhal
Maddie - Oliver Button is a Sissy

What do we notice?

We like different kinds of books!

Some of us like the same books!

▶ Emily created this chart with children to get a sense of the books everyone was interested in. It shows early interest and will expand over time.

◀ Bella decided to make a list of her favorite kinds of books so far, and Reiley explored *The Bad Seed*.

What If You Could Choose to Learn More About Yourself as a Reader?

Readers Choose Books They Can and Want to Read

Now that kids have learned more about the kinds of books they're interested in, Emily introduces these guiding questions as a way for children to refine their choices even more:

- *Am I interested in this book?*

- *Can I read most of the words?*

- *Do I understand most of the ideas?*

- *Does this book give me something to think and talk about?*

The questions are posted on the wall for easy reference, and small takeaway copies are available to any child who needs one.

✉ ✉ ✉

But there are no hard and fast rules. Choosing books depends on what the child is working toward. Keep in mind these questions as you support children in making their choices:

▶ Could a book that's easy to read be just right for a child working on fluency?

▶ Could a book above a child's level be just right for a child if he has extensive background knowledge about its content and/or is highly motivated to read it?

▶ Could a book be just right for a child working on comprehension if the words are easy to read but the content is challenging?

▶ Could a book be just right for a child working on decoding if [they know] most of the words, but not all of them, and the content is easy to understand?

▶ Could a challenging book be just right for the child who is highly motivated to read it?

▶ Could a book that's easy to read be just right for the child who needs to build background knowledge for a specific topic?

(From *Reading with Meaning*, Second Edition by Debbie Miller, copyright © 2012, reproduced with permission of Stenhouse Publishers. www.stenhouse.com)

▲ For children who need/want more support and practice, Emily explicitly teaches this questioning process in small groups.

◀ Jaycee and Kahlil use their personal takeaway copies of the questions to help them decide.

Right now I
like piggie and
elephant and the
barbie books.
they are fun to
read and they
kind of take
me on a little
advenchur and
I can read
all of the
words.

① I see a book that looks good!
② I pick it up→Open it!
③ I read some of the words
④ If I get stuck on a lot of words→I put it away
⑤then I get another book and try again!

I think that this looks good!

this is not good for me yet

▲ Children share their early reflections and processes for how to choose books.

Right now
capfain under pants
is too hard for me
because I don't
under stand what is
happenning.

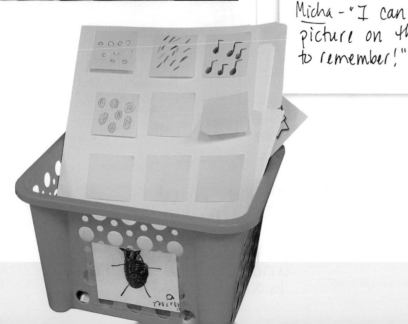

✱Micha Conference

- Had all Splat the Cat books Spread out

- "Mrs. Callahan! I got ALL of these books! there are 12 in the library! I already read one today and I'm going to read them ALL!"

Me- (thought about Questions when choosing books)
   - 'So it sounds like you're interested... What else?' - read the words? -understand ideas? -things to talk about?

Micha - "I can read ALL the words and I think Splat the Cat is really funny..." (retold book he'd just read)

Me- 'How are you going to keep track?'
✱ I had sticky notes - offered these as a way? ———→ He decided to put on
   Q- what could you   folder
   do when you finish
   one?

Micha - "I can draw a little picture on the sticky note to remember!"

LOVE! I figured he'd say 'tear one off! as a visual countdown ↳ this way is better!

↳ Confidence/Motivation is growing!!!

▲ Emily centers children in conferences, too. Simply saying, "What else?" and "How will you keep track?" helps Micha figure out what he wants to do.

I used to not be into reading but now I'm the kind of kid who reads books!!!

By micha

▲ When children share their work with everyone, confidence and agency grows!

He just keeps going!
Noticings - he's taking his time and being so thoughtful about what he chooses to draw on each sticky note → he decides what will help him remember ♡

My goal is to Ried all of the pig and eluth ent.

Books!

Waiting is not easy! I thot that even elfent had to wat he sow it and he riegreti cus it was Botf!

Elephants cannot Dance! Gerald even codint Do Dance But he still tride and he didint have a good day. But he had a good time cus people wut to lrn from him and I thot that was swet.

can I play Too? I thot that pige tot that thay can. not giv up. so thay hot a I beu, She playt whith the shace as the Ball.

We are in a Book! thay Didint whut the book to not end But they had a idu so they Did it!

▲ Inspired by Micha, this child puts her own spin on goal setting!

Readers Talk About Books

Just as we talk about books we're reading or have read, Emily makes time and space for kids to talk about books too! When she asked them, "What opportunities do you have to talk about books during the day?" a few children decided to share "all the ways" in pictures!

And when asked why "talking with each other" matters, kids responded that you talk so you can:

- connect with other people
- know more about what you think
- get ideas for books you want to read/recommend books to others
- help each other figure something out
- make new friends
- share who you are/learn who you are
- and—the more you talk, the more you know what you know.

Partner Talk

▼ "What are you reading?" "I'm thinking . . ." "I wonder . . ." "I feel . . ." "What if . . . ?"

Share and Reflection Circles

▶ "I tried something new today. Here's what happened . . ." "Can you talk more about that?" "I'm reading this great new series and I think some of you would really like it." "I'm learning I'm the kind of reader who . . ."

Book Clubs

▼ "I noticed that this character is kind of like . . ." "I wonder why . . ." "What does the author want us to remember forever?" "I don't get this part . . ." "I love this line because . . ."

Read-Alouds

▼ Kids turn and talk about big ideas in response to books their teacher reads aloud.

Walk-Arounds

▲ "What are you reading? What's it about?" "Have you read . . . ?" "Could you let me borrow that book when you're done?"

Gallery Walks

▲ In this instance, children each placed on their table a book that gave them something to think and talk about. They attached a sticky note to the cover to share their thinking, serving to inspire later conversations and new book choices.

Conferences

▲ "Can you say more about that?" "How does that make you feel?" "How are you growing as a reader?" "What do you think might be next for you?"

Readers Make Their Thinking Visible

We invite children to make their thinking visible because it's a means to a deeper understanding of both content (what they're learning) and themselves as learners (how they learn).

But something curious has happened over time—when children are routinely given two- or three-column notes, story frames, and/or writing prompts, we've boxed in their thinking and their learning. Literally.

But what might happen if children were invited to invent their own ways of putting their thinking on the page? Take a look at all the ways children made their thinking visible—and deepened their understanding—in the pages that follow.

"Fostering thinking requires making thinking visible" (Ritchhart and Perkins 2008, 58). This is how we learn more about what and how children are thinking, learning, and feeling, giving us insight into how to support and connect with them in genuine, wholehearted ways.

▲ When children are trying something new, we find that being together in one space is often reassuring and helpful for some. Kids watch, talk, try out, and learn together in a no-pressure, collaborative, and supportive way.

Why I make my Thinking Visible
- So I can Remember What I Read
- So I can Remember the Lesson (fiction + true stories)
- Remember what I Learned (nonfiction + true stories)
- So I can teach others
- So I can Look Back at It & add to it
  Synthesizing ✓
- Because my teacher asked me to
- Write down inferences
- Determinations
- What if?
- It confused me...
- I don't understand...
- How could...
- Something crazy happened
- I Believe...

▲ "How are you using sticky notes to make your thinking visible?"

"I'm the Kind of Kid Who..."

I make my thinking visable because I want people to see what I see.

I ♡ this BOOK cuz... ??? I disagree... on Paper

◄ Kendell has so much thinking he wanted to use a big chart to fit in "all my thinking."

a bad Bone   Jumping for exercise   Stayty rules

● don't try to do a flip on feat. ● #Land have got hurt. ● Jump # Jumping Jacks ● don't Jump on the fast the metal on ## Jump on the not metal part ② Jump after Lor3 Jump ③ Dont risky flips.

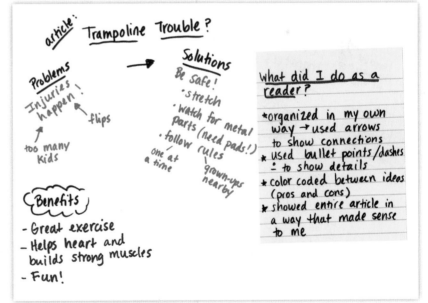

article: Trampoline Trouble?

Problems
Injuries happen! ← flips
← too many Kids

Solutions
Be safe!
• stretch
• watch for metal parts (need pads!)
• follow rules
  • one at a time
  • grown-ups nearby

Benefits
- Great exercise
- Helps heart and builds strong muscles
- Fun!

What did I do as a reader?
*organized in my own way → used arrows to show connections
* used bullet points/dashes - to show details
* color coded between ideas (pros and cons)
* showed entire article in a way that made sense to me

▲ Emily and Jericho were both interested in reading the same article about trampolines. They made a plan to read it on their own, make their thinking visible, and meet again to compare their processes.

▲ Kendall was inspired by the book *A Bike Like Sergio's*, and wanted to share her learning with the world in a "Good Vibes" book. She knows just what she needs.

▲ Kids love minibooks! They fit in their hands and are versatile, accessible, and perfect for making thinking and learning visible. (To make a minibook all you need to do is cut several pieces of paper in half, fold, and staple!)

▲ During a social studies unit on American symbols, Emily read aloud a short article about the Statue of Liberty and asked kids, "How will you put your thinking and learning on the page? A note to educators: What does this image reveal about children's thinking? What decisions did they make?"

Dear Jericho,
I noticed that Kashton
is also really into poetry!
I'm wondering if you
might want to share
your ideas with each
other? Let me know
if you do!
♡ Love,
Mrs. Callahan

it just feels
good to get
all my think
down in my
think ing chart
I like to make
it feels good to
share my
♡ think ing
with everyone

▲ During independent reading, Jericho discovered he loved poetry. The more he read, the more he noticed the moves poets make. When a poem was really good, he said it had "gravy" and "waves." He made his thinking visible on this chart, and it wasn't long before he began creating his own poems that were brimming with gravy and waves!

CIRCLE of FRIENDS

Kindness Bar

Kindness kept GROWING!

In CIRCLE of FRIENDS the mom is nice to the boy, then the boy's nice to a homeless man and then the homeless man was nice to a BIRD-wait...you know what?
I realized it is a cause and effect!

Kindness

The stranger
The colors...
the bigger tho
kindness

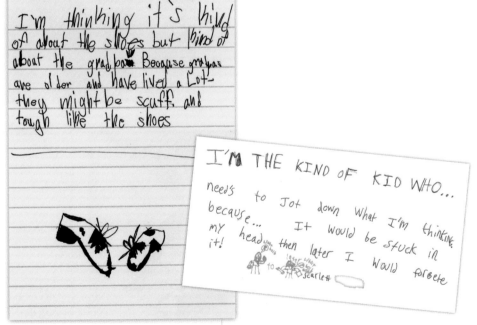

I'm thinking it's kind of about the shoes but kind of about the grad pa? Because grad pas are older and have lived a Lot- they might be scuff and tough like the shoes

I'M THE KIND OF KID WHO...

needs to jot down what I'm thinking because... It would be stuck in my head, then later I would forgete it!

scarlet

▲ "When learners speak, draw, or write their ideas, they deepen their cognition" (Ritchhart and Perkins 2008).

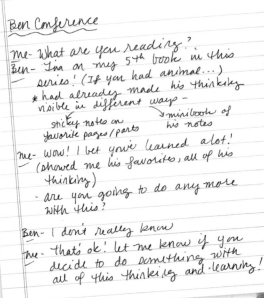

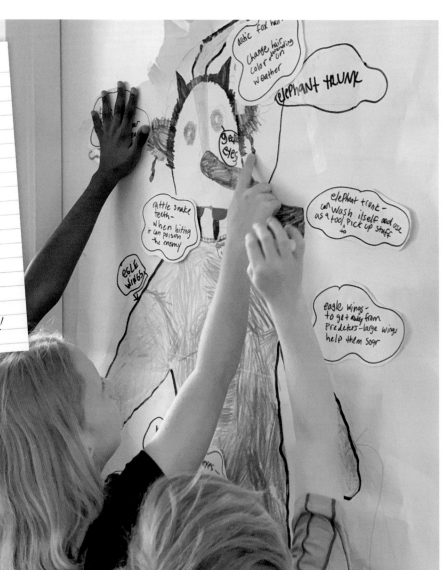

A few days after his conference with Emily, Ben had an idea! "I want to make a big 'superhuman' to show all my favorite parts and what I learned about them!" He asked an interested friend to trace his body on a big piece of paper, and they were off. A few others asked to join, and Ben agreed. They taped their superhuman out in the hall for all to see and learn.

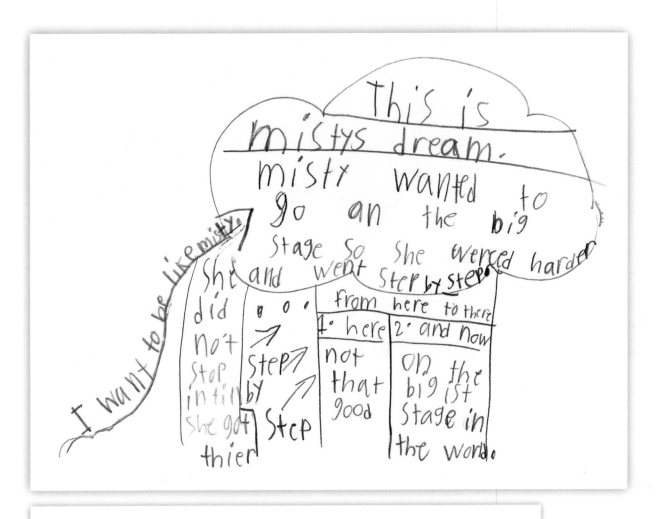

Each Kindness

This book shows my regret.

We also need to be a class family and be nice to every one.

I always try to be nice

But sometimes only the mean comes out.

"Books offer children 'mirrors' into their own lives, helping them learn more about who they are, who they are becoming, and who they want to be" (Bishop 1990).

Readers Recommend Books

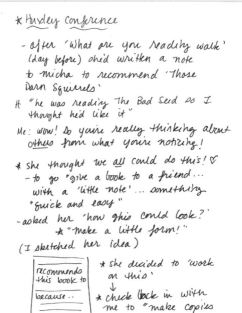

Huxley Conference

- after 'What are you reading walk'
  (day before) she'd written a note
  to micha to recommend 'Those
  Darn Squirrels'
H: "he was reading The Bad Seed so I
  thought he'd like it"
Me: Wow! So you're really thinking about
  others from what you're noticing!

★ she thought we all could do this! ♡
  - to go "give a book to a friend...
    with a 'little note'... something
    "quick and easy"
  - asked her 'how this could look?'
    ★ "make a little form!"
(I sketched her idea)

recommends
this book to
↓
because..

★ she decided to 'work
  on this'
↓
★ check back in with
  me to "make copies
  to put near the class
  library!" ♡

Huxley - I wanted
to recommend this
book to you
because it is
kind and sweet
like you and
you like those kind
of books ♡
love, maddie

recommends
this book to...
_____
because...
_____
_____
_____
_____

▲ We love book recommendations, and
we imagine most of you do too. So do
kids! Huxley decides to take charge.

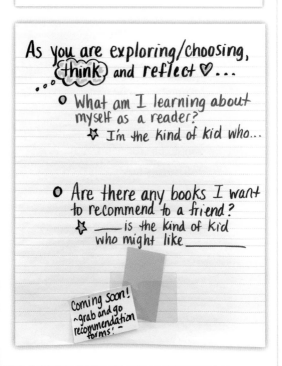

As you are exploring/choosing,
(think) and reflect ♡...

○ What am I learning about
  myself as a reader?
  ☆ I'm the kind of kid who...

○ Are there any books I want
  to recommend to a friend?
  ☆ ____ is the kind of kid
  who might like _____

Coming soon!
~ grab and go
recommendation
forms!~

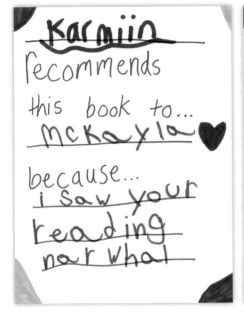

Karmiin
recommends
this book to...
McKayla ♥

because...
i saw your
reading
nor whal

Aubree
recommends
(write! write! write!)
this book to...
Mrs. Callahan

because...
you love teaching
writing and all
things poetry ♥♥
☺ ☺ ☺

Kids recommend books in a variety of ways. Even Mrs. Callahan gives and receives recommendations!

Dear Kahlil,
You mentioned during our share circle yesterday that you've read, I Am Enough two times! Did you know Grace Byers has another book (I Believe I Can)? I think you might enjoy this one too!
♡ Mrs. Callahan

Dear; Aubree... I think you would like this book because... it's like poetry and I know you like poetry! ♡ Scarlett

I, Kaybr recommends this book to: YOU-tomiin because... you like princeses a spise

I'm the kind of kid who shops for myself and I also shop for others. I know what my friends like to read so I think about books for them too ♥.

Jory John is the kind of person who tells you to Love the way you live

Please keep the Jory John Books in here— author study in progress! ♥ THANKS!

Readers Participate in Book Clubs

Are you in a book club? Do you also talk about books with friends, family, and colleagues in a more spontaneous way?

Emily's kids do both of these things too! And though she hadn't really thought about starting book clubs yet, she began to notice kids coming together on their own to talk about books—some kids naturally got together because they noticed they were reading the same book or series, others wanted to dig deeper into a read-aloud with a partner, and still others simply wanted to read beside someone and explore ideas along the way. These "spontaneous book clubs" happened naturally, without fuss or fanfare. Some last a day, others three or four or sometimes more—these get-togethers are dynamic and flexible. (How do kids get to know what everyone is reading? Through walk-arounds and gallery walks, reflection and share circles, oral and artistic responses, and of course just being close together! They're immersed in a culture of readers and reading!)

As time went on, some kids wanted something more—they wanted to be in a "real" book club that we organize. This was the mission of a small group of kids who wanted to be in a book club to "study all the Jory John books." Emily had read aloud *The Bad Seed, The Good Egg, The Cool Bean,* and *The Great Eggscape,* and they just couldn't get enough. They just knew there was more thinking between those covers! So they got themselves an empty tub, filled it with the books they wanted from the Jory John tub in their classroom library, and made a plan: "Let's reread all the books and talk about what we are thinking and learning." And just like that, they began! No fuss or fanfare here either!

And, of course, it wasn't long before other kids wanted to be in book clubs too.

◄ Kids create their own "book-club tub" that they can take anywhere! What's inside? Books, sticky notes, blank paper, a calendar, markers . . .

Things we are noticing/Patterns we are finding in Jory John books...

* "He wants you to be mindful - to notice, change, and live a better life."   - Bella

* "Most all the characters start off as complainers but then they start to change" -Demi

* "Each character has their own distinct personality that you can see right away" - Reiley

The Great Eggscape
I noticed...

When you lose a friend and they are gone for some time it is time to look for him. It is like your buds really need you. And you need them♡

In the Good Egg it shows you it is a good way to be kind—and never leave your buds—Your buds are your everything

Emily met with the Jory John kids to find out more about where they were and what they might need. They had spent time writing their thinking on sticky notes, and through their discussion, she captured their current thinking about Jory John and his books.

The Cool Bean
I noticed...
That this book shows that you Don't have to Be 'cool' to get friends. It is cool to be kind. That's how you Be a cool friend.
            —Bella

Reflecting: Where Are We Now?

▲ Isaiah

I'm the kind of Kid who likes to read. It all started with The Alien Next Door. And then I started reading them all. I could read the words and it had pictures. I read all 8 in two weeks! I started to read a Lot more and Just Love reading. I learned that it takes a good Series for me.

▲ Elijah

Chase, Elijah, Isaiah, and Taylin share their reading journeys in different ways!

▲ Chase

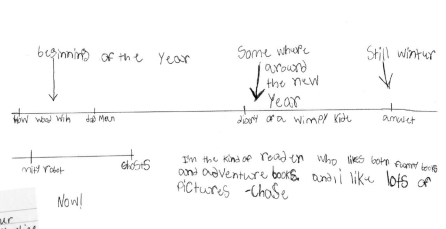

beginning of the year

Some where around the new year

Still wintur

How wead with dob Man

diory of a wimpy Kide

amulet

mity robot

ghostS

Now!

I'm the kind of reader who likes both funny books and adventure books. and i like lots of pictures -Chase

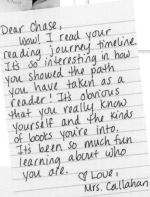

Dear Chase,
Wow! I read your reading journey timeline. It's so interesting in how you showed the path you have taken as a reader! It's obvious that you really know yourself and the kinds of books you're into. It's been so much fun learning about who you are.
Love,
Mrs. Callahan

"I'm the Kind of Kid Who…"

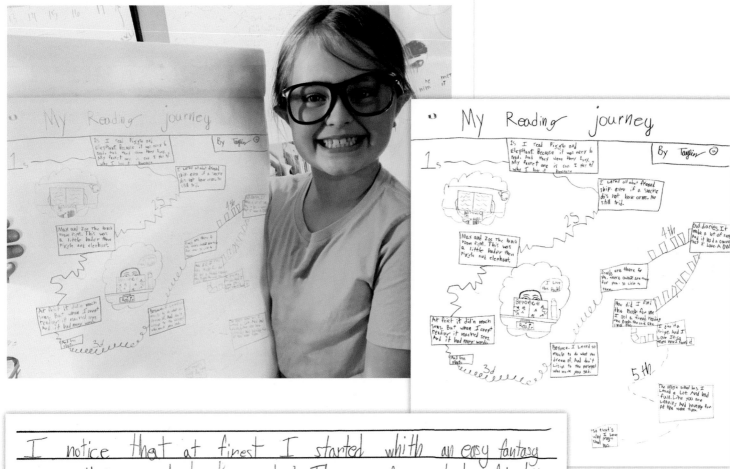

I notice that at finest I started whith an easy fantasy series that I already Knew about. They were funny and about friendship and made me happy. Then I got into harder realistic fiction Books that still taught me about friendship. Then I started reading inspiring books like true stories that inspire me to do things that I Love like follow a dream. Then I started to read a harden series. It was like a huge step up because I could read bigger and harder books. I'm the kind of reader who likes so many different kinds of BOOK!

▲ Taylin's latest reflection and thinking about the Beyoncé book that inspired her.

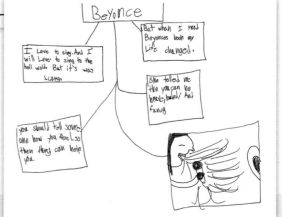

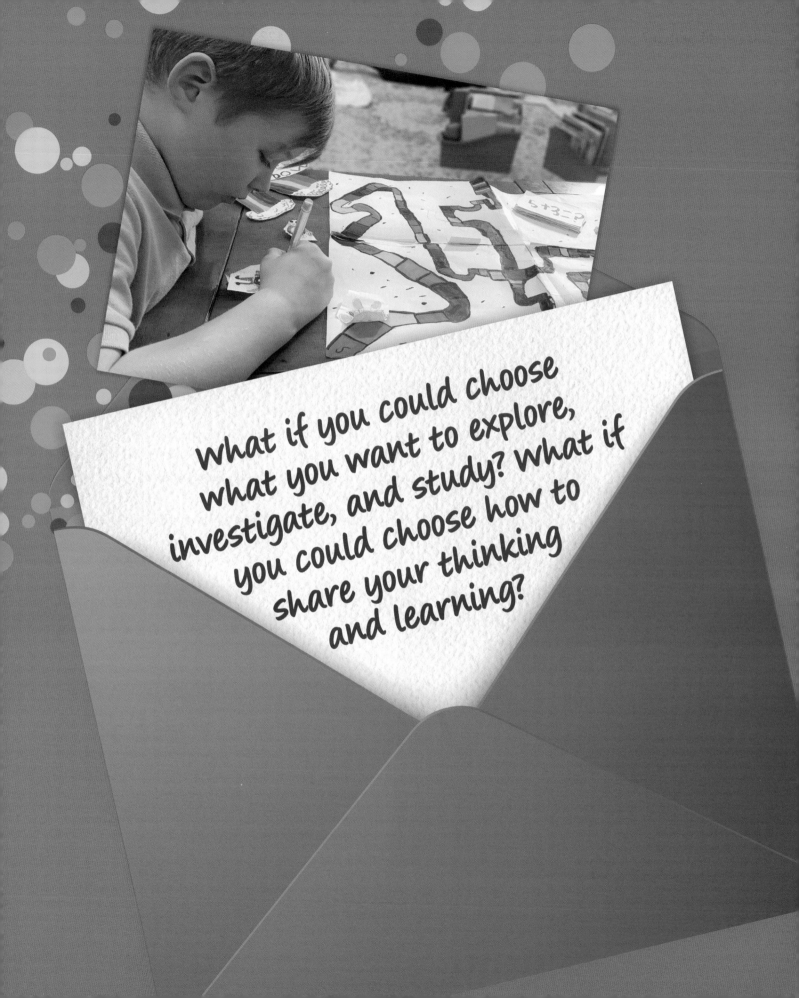

What if you could choose what you want to explore, investigate, and study? What if you could choose how to share your thinking and learning?

Getting Started
What Might You Need to Know?

Vision

We imagine children spread out across the room, at tables, on the floor in twos, threes, and small groups, investigating topics they care about. Their arms are full, carrying stacks of books, iPads, notebooks, chart paper, sticky notes, blank paper, manipulatives, and a range of writing tools. We see smiles on their faces—they're happy, engaged, and looking forward to sharing their new thinking and learning in a variety of ways.

About This Invitation

This invitation puts into play those that have come before—children have explored materials and thought about where they learn and work best; they know more about how they make their thinking visible and who they are as readers. And now it's time to put everything together! It serves as a beautiful testament to how kids have developed a more visible, deeper sense of learner identity and agency.

You'll notice Emily launched this invitation during her thirty-minute choice time. It's an unstructured time, giving children sizable chunks of time (across days) to dig into a topic they care deeply about, as well as figure out how they want to share what they've learned and with whom. But social studies or science could also be a launching option, especially when kids get to choose what they want to learn more about in those areas.

You might find that some children might not be as interested as others in this invitation on the day you launch it—they may be in the middle of a book club, math study, an art project, or something else. (This is choice time after all!) But they are always welcome to join in when/if the time is right for them.

> what if you could choose what you want to explore, investigate, and study? What if you could choose how to share your thinking and learning?

Research

Lev Vygotsky tells us, "It must not be forgotten that the basic law of children's creativity is that its value lies not in its results, not in the product of creation, but in the process itself. It is not important what children create, but that they do create, that they exercise and implement their creative imagination" (2004).

When Will I Launch It?
When Else Can We Practice?

Science

Choice Time

What if you could choose what you want to explore, investigate, and study? What if you could choose how to share your thinking and learning?

Social Studies

Reading

Math

Writing

A Note from Emily . . .

I want to clarify that this invitation isn't about a giant, full-blown research project that all kids have to be a part of. This invitation is meant to be low-stress (but it's not a free-for-all either). When you offer this invitation to children, some will accept right away, and others might decide to jump in later (and that's OK!). If children decide to explore, investigate, and study something they care about, they get to work at their own pace, create their own timelines, and learn about their own processes. Of course, some children will need us—but before we immediately jump in to support them, we need to stand back to actually see what will happen, to observe what they do, and to invite them to explore. We can't know what they'll need until we let them try. This isn't about teacher-created rubrics and due dates—it's about choice and centering children.

Planning
What Was Our Plan? How Did We Start?

Guiding Questions

1. Why might this invitation matter?

As Annie Murphy Paul (2013) described, "Interest effectively turbocharges our thinking. When we're interested in what we're learning, we pay closer attention; we process the information more efficiently; we employ more effective learning strategies, such as engaging in critical thinking, making connections between old and new knowledge, and attending to deep structure instead of surface features. When we're interested in a task, we work harder and persist longer, bringing more of our self-regulatory skills into play."

2. What books, resources, and materials might children need?

If a child chooses to accept this invitation, you'll need to support them in finding as many books/materials for whatever topic/area they wish to explore. They can check with the librarian too! And make sure supplies are well stocked and ready to go.

3. When might I launch it?

__Reading __Writing __Math __Social Studies __Science
X̲ Choice Time Or__

4. What might I say?

Everyone, you know how we have units where we all explore the same topic? Like we've had units on matter and energy, plants and animals, and landforms, right?

But think about this: What if you could choose to explore, investigate, and study any topic you want to . . . one that you are really interested in, something you truly care about? You could choose to learn on your own, with a partner, or in a small group. You could get to decide what you want to learn more about, how things will work, and how you want to share what you've learned with others. And as always, if you need me, you know I would help you any way I can.

You already know about investigating and researching a topic, so you'd be using many of the same thinking strategies you know about already, like asking questions, figuring out what you think is important, and synthesizing information. And now, you'd be using them to help you explore, investigate, or study a topic you choose. What do you think: What are some things you might want to explore?

And one last thing . . . I know some of you are in the middle of other things—no worries! You can jump into this invitation when and if the time is right for you. Off you go. I'm excited to learn with you!

5. What reflective questions might I ask?

- "Are you learning anything new about how you learn and/or what you need?"

- "Is there something new you've learned about your topic that surprised you?"

- "Is there something you've learned about yourself, or someone else, that you didn't know before?"

- "Do you have any ideas yet about how you'll share what you've learned?"

- "How is your group (or partnership) working? Do you need any help from me?"

6. How might I know what kids need and how they're growing? How might I share with them what I've learned?

- Kidwatch, listen in, study what kids make, confer

- Through personal notes to children; whole-group and small-group reflection circles; conferring; and short, in-the-moment conversations

Launching Chart

> ☑ • What if you could choose what to explore, investigate, and study?
> • What if you could choose how to share your thinking and learning?
>
> ☆ Let's imagine...
>
> | | |
> |---|---|
> | ○ What will I explore? | ○ How will I make my thinking and learning visible along the way? |
> | ○ What do I want to share with others? | ○ How will I share it? What will I need? |

▲ This chart will reflect children's thinking and learning throughout the invitation.

Planning Notes

* Launching → ⟨cloud⟩ - choosing what to explore, investigate, and study...
- choosing how to share thinking and learning...⟩

- Offered invitation -

→ What might you want to explore?

* Caitlin, Riley, Isaiah, Micha
- saving animals
pollution | cats | video game

* Gray, Isabel, Tia, Faith Loves
"We're really into wordless books!"
↳ Do more thinking??!

* Nora
"I just checked out a book about mermaids!"

* Request more wordless books from the library!!

* Kendall
"I just watched a movie about Helen Keller - I want to learn more!"

* Remind her later about books we have in our library
↳ Books about strong women!

* Aiden - mentioned idea of soccer to Gavin...
"maybe later..." (had just started a new series - wanted to keep reading)

* JJ - dinosaurs!

* Demi -
"I'm already in a books club right now..."

* Reminded... It's OK to decide later →
meet with interested kids tomorrow ☺

◄ Emily's notes as children turn and talk about what they are interested in.

Digging In: What Did We Try? What Happened? What Did We Learn?

A note to readers—On the pages that follow, you'll learn the stories and processes of kids who came together to explore something they cared about and how they decided to share their thinking and learning. Get ready to meet the Mermaids, the NFL Kids, the Wordless Wonders, the Math Teachers, and Anuli and her "Words to Live By!"

Meet the Mermaids!

Kendall, Nora, and Grace were reading books about mermaids—they were in the midst of a mythology unit in reading—and they couldn't help but wonder, "Are mermaids really real?" They shared their question during share time, and several others wanted to join in—they had the same question, as well as some compelling reasoning: One had actually seen a "real mermaid" at the aquarium, and another mentioned that they sell outfits for mermaids at Target. So, their little group grew—they read and talked and read and talked some more, making their thinking and learning visible on a big roll of paper.

As Gambrell, Morrow, and Pressley (2007) tell us, "Comprehension processes must be employed in real time, and the best evidence of their use is students' responses as they read, not in response to questions (or worksheets) afterward. There is no evidence that a steady diet of completing such post-reading sheets, in fact, leads to active reading."

▲ Even more thinking!

Kids couldn't wait to tally their surveys! Final count? Fourteen circled yes, mermaids are real; seven circled no.

The group couldn't conclusively say that mermaids were real, but they couldn't (wouldn't) say they weren't either (And we believe it's entirely appropriate to believe in mermaids when you're seven or eight!)

Video 7–1 » To hear Kendall's reflection about being part of the mermaid group, listen in to her conference with Emily over Zoom.

See page ix to access the online video.

Name: Jack
So What Do You think?
1. Real or Not Real

2. Why
because I herd myths and I saw pictures and I belief in mermaids

▲ Nora synthesized what she'd learned about mermaids by making a book she called *The Mermaid Song and Other Poems*.

Meet the NFL Boys!

Friends Atticus and Anthony love football. Especially the Kansas City Chiefs! At the time of this invitation, the playoffs were coming up, and they noticed a problem: "Not that many know how the playoffs work—how can they not know?" To fix this problem they decided to write an article that would help people out. They wanted to share how important the playoffs are, so maybe people "might learn to love football as much as we do!"

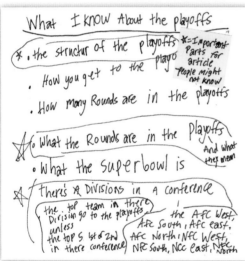

▲ They organized what they already knew.

▶ And they included a large and colorful graphic in their article titled "How Brackets Work." (Yay Chiefs!)

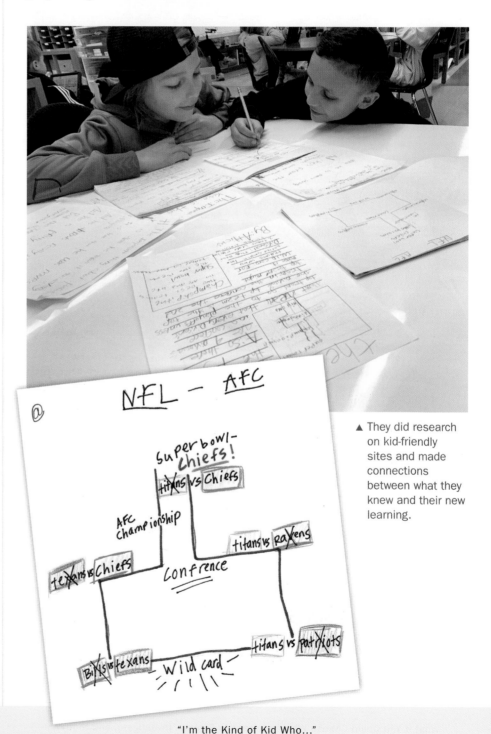

▲ They did research on kid-friendly sites and made connections between what they knew and their new learning.

▶ Atticus and Anthony get it: "Find a way to share. It doesn't have to be a big deal!"

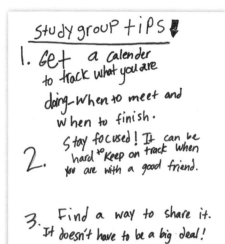

study group tips ↓

1. Get a calender to track what you are doing-when to meet and when to finish.

2. Stay focused! It can be hard to keep on track when you are with a good friend.

3. Find a way to share it. It doesn't have to be a big deal!

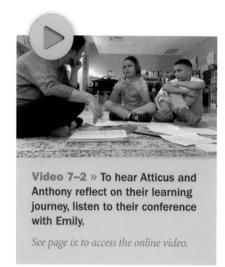

Video 7–2 » **To hear Atticus and Anthony reflect on their learning journey, listen to their conference with Emily.**

See page ix to access the online video.

◀ And . . . they're back at it! They were also immersed in a craft study in writers' workshop, where they were learning how authors use obvious text structures to engage readers. They read (and loved) *The Important Book* by Margaret Wise Brown and decided to embark on another collaborative project about their beloved Kansas City Chiefs.

The Important Thing About the Chiefs By: Atticus & Anthony

Tyrann Mathieu
Page 5

The important thing about Tyrann Mathieu is that he's the Honeybadger. It is true that he was named the most valuable player at the 2011 SEC championship game (where he earned the nickname the honey badger). And this was for his tenacious ability to play extremely tough football against much larger opponents as well as his knack for making big plays. And he also gets a lot of interceptions. But the important thing about Tyrann Mathieu is that he's the Honeybadger.

Chris Jones
Page 3

The important thing about Chris Jones is that he gets a lot of sacks and blocks. It is true that he is a great defensive tackle. He puts a lot of pressure on the quarterback to force him to throw or run. And his pressure makes the quarterbacks throw worse. But the important thing about Chris Jones is that he gets a lot of sacks and blocks.

Walls That Teach

This "What might I try? What might I need?" space is an example of a wall (cabinet!) that teaches. Anytime a child feels "stuck" or in need of support and/or inspiration, it offers ideas to help them sustain. Cocreated with (and mostly by) children, you'll notice several sections:

- **Planning:** What will I share? How will I plan?

- **Sharing and/or teaching others:** What are some things I might want to keep in mind?

- **Inspiration:** What have others done that I might try?

- **Assessment** How did it go?

Emily also provides small takeaway copies of some examples, just in case kids want their own to keep.

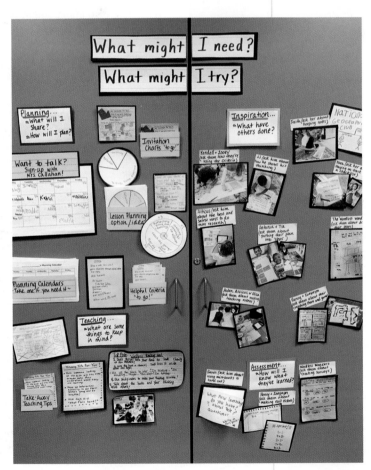
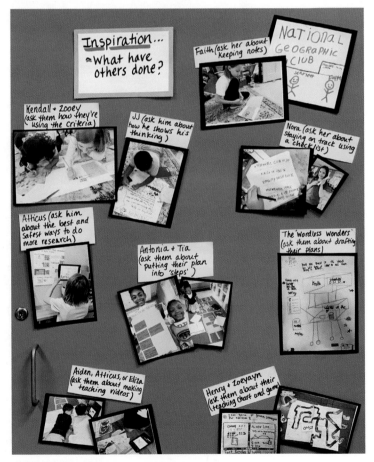

▲ Using these examples, a child might ask themselves, "Hmm. What did other kids try? What might make sense for me? Is there something I want to learn more about? Who could I go talk to?"

During conferences (see photo at right) or when she's listening in, Emily sometimes releases responsibility to children by referring them to the "What might I try? What might I need?" space.

- "You're realizing you have too much information here and it's feeling a little too big? OK, let's figure out what's most important."

- "You have a topic but you don't know your next steps? OK, let's brainstorm a little bit, what are you wondering? What do you want to figure out?"

- "You're not quite sure how to start? OK, let's get a calendar and map it out."

- "You've done your research and you want to teach a lesson to others, but aren't quite sure how? OK, let's look at this planning circle and try to figure it out."

- "You have formed your group, but aren't quite sure who should take on which role? OK, what support do you need with collaborating?"

- "You're not quite sure how to make your thinking visible? OK, let's revisit the ways we can do this."

▲ Zooey and Kendall used a takeaway copy of Demi's "criteria" to help them think through their plan. (Thanks, Demi!)

▲ Maddie signs up for a conference with Mrs. Callahan.

Meet the Wordless Wonders!

During a conference with Gray during independent reading, Gray shared, "Faith and I just don't get it—why isn't anybody reading wordless books except for us? We think they are so good! And big kids and really everyone needs to read them too because wordless books aren't only for babies, and they have a lot of things to teach us." Gray asked some friends if they'd like to dig into wordless books too. They made a plan to meet to share what they were noticing, learning, and wondering.

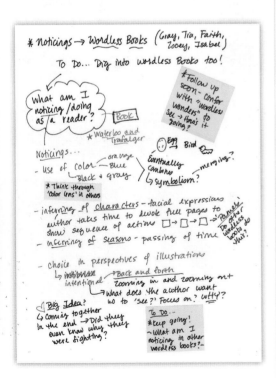

◀ Emily, too, looked closely at wordless books and recorded what she was noticing and thinking. This kind of work gives perspective and depth to her interactions and conversations with children.

▼ After a few days, Emily saw this stack of kid work at their table. It looked beautiful, and they were certainly busy, but what were they *doing*? She conferred with them to find out.

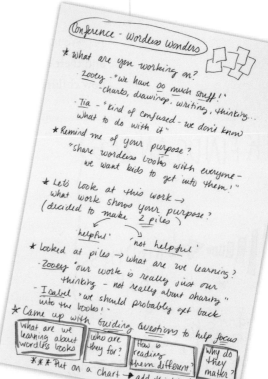

◄ Ah! Now she knows more about what the Wordless Wonders need!

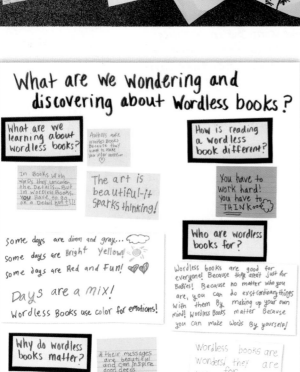

And they're off! In this short conference (see Emily's conferring notes), she gave children just the right amount of support—not too much, not too little—to energize, focus, and sustain their work. (And the guiding questions? Genius!) Now that they are back on track, they dug back into their wordless books and added their thinking to the newly made chart. (Check out even more of their work on the following pages.)

We noticed a big difference between these responses (see images below) and their earlier efforts on the previous page. The earlier responses were about how children were making meaning as they read. But the work on this page is more intentional, created specifically to share what wordless books can offer readers. (Did their earlier work influence this work? We think so!) These are examples of what can happen when we give children time and freedom to make choices about how they'll share what they've learned. A worksheet or organizer could never generate responses like these! This is about trust. This is about time. And this is about believing in the brilliance of children.

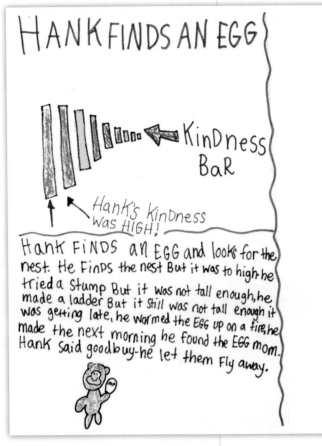

What's in their cart? What will readers need?

- Wordless books in a tub/bottom shelf (Why? "Readers need to choose the ones they want to read.")

- Kendall's suggestions for reading wordless books (Why? "We want readers to know that you do a lot of the same things you do when you read books with words, especially thinking!")

- Sticky notes and pencils to keep track of thinking (Why? "We want readers to slow down and be thoughtful.")

- Faith's survey questions (Why? "We want to find out what readers think about wordless books!")

- Book checkout form (Why? "In case they want to take some home to share with their families.")

- List of wordless books (Why? "In case kids or maybe grown-ups want to read more.")

▲ In the end, the Wordless Wonders realized that the best way for them to share with the world what they've learned about wordless books is to invite people to discover and experience them for themselves: "Let's make a cart of wordless books to take around the school!" Check out how they envision their cart-on-the-go. What do you notice? What do you wonder?

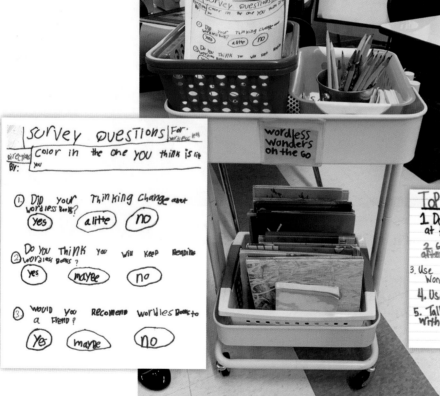

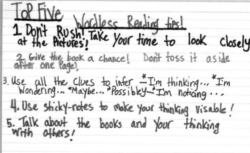

▲ Faith, Kendall, and Gray think carefully about what needs to go on their cart. They, and the rest of the Wordless Wonders, have the sense of agency within them—they believe they are the kind of kids who can work together to make their vision a reality.

Meet the Math Teachers!

Zoeyayn and Henry were math enthusiasts—they're always excited to try out new math strategies and reflect on what they're learning. When Emily offered this invitation, they couldn't stop talking and thinking about how to share some of their best math strategies with first graders. But first, they wrote a note to Miss Parker, their beloved first-grade teacher, to set up a meeting to find out what strategies the kids in her class needed most.

> Dear miss Parker,
> We have an idea
> about teaching math!
> Can we come up
> during lunch to
> talk and ask
> you some
> questions?
> * Just email Mrs. Callahn
> ♥ Henry and Zoeyayn

> PLAN 1st grade
> 1. Use tools to modle Promlums
> 2.

> * What subject? Math!!! + addition
>
> * What's your learning target?
> ⊙ I can use stratigies to help me with addition
>
> * How will you teach it?
> Chart with boxes! ← stratigies
>
> * How will you know what they've learned?
> try out a stratigy with a problem

▶ Once they knew what they wanted to teach, Henry and Zoeyayn began to think about how they'd teach it. They asked for a conference with Emily. "Will you show us what you do when you plan lessons?" She shared a few questions she thinks about (in orange), and they wrote their ideas in blue.

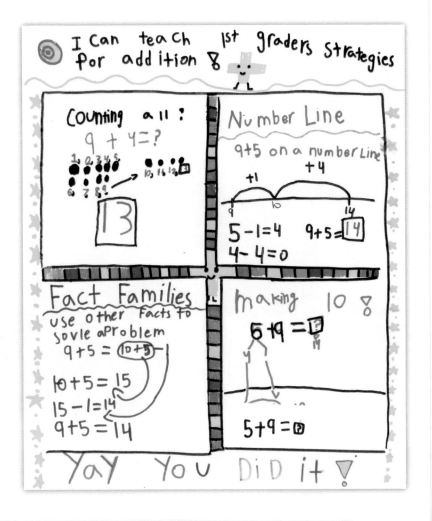

I Can teach 1st graders Strategies for addition & +

Counting all:
9 + 4 = ?
1 2 3 4 5
⬤⬤⬤⬤⬤ → ⬤ 10, 11, 12, 13
⬤⬤⬤⬤
6 7 8 9
13

Number Line
9+5 on a number Line
+1   +4
9   10   14
5 - 1 = 4   9 + 5 = 14
4 - 4 = 0

Fact Families
use other facts to sovle a problem
9 + 5 = 10 + 5
10 + 5 = 15
15 - 1 = 14
9 + 5 = 14

making 10 &
6 + 9 = 15
5 + 9 = 15

Yay You DiD it!

◀ After meeting with Miss Parker they settled on these four strategies. What do you notice about their chart? What do they know about how to share what they know with first graders?

Name _____
Miss Parker had 7 pieces of candy. Mr. Martin gave her 5 more. How many does she have now?
↓ Solve! Show your strategy!

exit ticket: show your strategy!
| 8+6 | 6+9 |

Henry & Zoeyayn's Calendar/Planning Template

Month: All months (except Spring Break)
*start after SB

Monday	Tuesday	Wednesday	Thursday	Friday
talk with ms. Parker / Plan New stradigie	Plan make stratiges	teach stradigies	Plan out story problems	Plan out story problems
make story problems	make story problems	teach story problem	plan sprint warm up	plan sprint warm up
make sprint warm up	make sprint warm up	sprint warm up / go over stradiges		
		play game!		

▲ They used a calendar to help them plan and designed a few exit tickets to learn more from their students: "What's working? What isn't?"

Instructions
Pick a character
Place it on Start
Draw a card
Solve the Problem
Move Your
Characters
get to the end
to win!

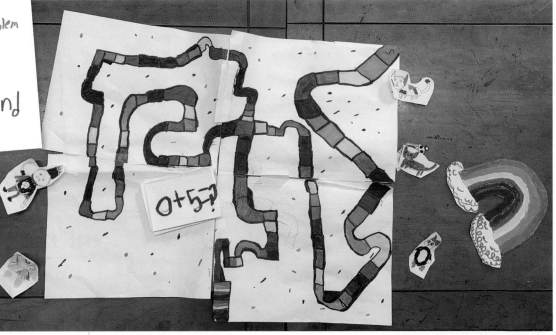

▲ Henry and Zoeyayn noticed that the first graders weren't really practicing as much as they thought they should. What to do? They decided to make a game to make it more fun and help them learn! They modeled their game after the children's classic "Candy Land," calling it "Add the Rainbow." Their game included a game board and pieces, instructions, and a game box for easy transport.

▲ It's game day! And Zoeyayn and Henry are ready. They have a plan, and here you see them in the thick of things, showing kids how to play. Come on. Does it get any better than this?!

#1 teaching strategies for addition

#3 Reflecting - going over learning

teach the game / exit ticket

PLAY the game

#2

Henry + Zoeyayn,
Thank you both <u>SO</u> <u>MUCH</u> for helping out in 1st grade. You've been so prepared and thanks to your effort, our students are <u>GROWING</u>! They love learning from such talented mathematicians, and can't wait until the next time. Thanks for showing them math can be <u>A LOT OF FUN</u>!
♡ Miss Parker

Video 7–3 » Henry and Zoeyayn just can't stop teaching! Listen in as Henry explains their upcoming plans for their first-grade mathematicians.

See page ix to access the online video.

▲ Miss Parker doesn't think so!

Reflecting: Where Are We Now?

Meet Anuli

From the day we met her, Anuli was the kind of kid who thought deeply about everything. She loved to talk and think about big ideas during read-alouds and in her own reading; she collected quotes that inspired her and kept them in a notebook she titled "Words to Live By." But the book that inspired her to write her own "Words to Live By" was *A Dictionary for a Better World* by Irene Latham and Charles Waters et al. She read that beautiful book over and over, and then she just couldn't stop writing. She shared her words with everyone, especially her like-minded former teacher, Miss Williams. Miss Williams encouraged her to take her favorite poems out of her notebook and share them with the world. And that's just what Anuli did! (Thank you, Anuli!)

And wouldn't it be something if Anuli's "Words to Live By" became the words the world lives by?

Anuli's words To Live By...
Belonging
When Someone is Down, cheer them up
When someone is alone, go say hi
Be the somebody that Blooms for her
and tells her that she Belongs
Be the someBody
for the someone

Anuli's Words to Live By...
Together
Acceptance is Discovering
that everyone is Different
in their own Kind of Way
You don't have to Be alone
You can Be With someone
that is the same in some
ways, But also Different too
and Just Because We're
Different, We can Still Be
in this together.

Anuli's Words To Live By...
Communities
When people everywhere
look at the night sky,
Different cultures
Different communities
Different Countries
Come together as

One Big Family

Anuli's Words To Live By...
Differences
Kenya Nigeria
My uncle told me, me and my cousins
are not the Same- One Wants to Be a
gamer and one Wants to Be a firefighter
I want to be a Doctor- DIVERSITY!
We are from Different parts of Africa-
DIVERSITY! My cousins are half Kenyon,
I'm half Nigerian- DIVERSITY!

WORKS CITED

Anderson, Mike. 2016. *Learning to Choose. Choosing to Learn.* Alexandria, VA: ASCD.

Bishop, Rudine Sims. 1990. "Mirrors, Windows, and Sliding Glass Doors." *Perspectives* 6 (3): ix-xi.

Brookhart, Susan M., and Alice Oakley. 2021. *How to Look at Student Work to Uncover Thinking.* Alexandria, VA: ASCD.

Cruz, M. Colleen. 2020. *Risk, Fail, Rise: A Teacher's Guide to Learning from Mistakes.* Portsmouth, NH: Heinemann

Dewey, John. 1907. *The School and Society.* Chicago: University of Chicago Press.

Dyson, Anne Haas. 1993. *Social Worlds of Children Learning to Write in an Urban Primary School.* New York: Teachers College Press.

Gambrell, Linda B., Lesley Mandell Morrow, and Michael Pressley, eds. 2007. *Best Practices in Literacy Instruction. 3rd ed.* New York: The Guilford Press.

Goodman, Y. M. 1985. "Kidwatching: Observing Children in the Classroom." In *Observing the Language Learner*, edited by A. Jagger and M. T. Smith-Burke, 9–18. Urbana, IL: NCTE and IRA.

Greene, Maxine. 1987. Commencement Address, Bank Street College, New York.

Guthrie, John, and Nicole Humenick. 2004. "Motivating Students to Read: Evidence for Classroom Practices That Increase Reading Motivation and Achievement." In *The Voice of Evidence in Reading Research*, edited by P. McDardle and V. Chhabra, 329–54. Baltimore, MD: Paul H. Brookes Publishing.

Johnston, Peter H. 2004. *Choice Words: How Our Language Affects Children's Learning.* Portland, ME: Stenhouse.

Kohn, Alfie. (@alfiekohn). 2021. "Tchrs who listen to kids' conversations, observe their projects, & read their writing don't need to use tests. But this assumes kids have a chance to converse, design projects, & write. If they just listen to lecs & do wksheets, there's not much authentic learning to BE assessed." Twitter, February 3, 2021, 9:11 a. m. https://twitter.com/alfiekohn/status/1356968510900097024.

MacKay, Susan Harris. 2021. *Story Workshop: New Possibilities for Young Writers.* Portsmouth, NH: Heinemann.

Miller, Debbie. 2012. *Reading with Meaning: Teaching Comprehension in the Primary Grades.* 2nd ed. Portland, ME: Stenhouse.

Paul, Annie Murphy. 2013. "How the Power of Interest Drives Learning." *KQED Mind/Shift* Nov. 4. https://www.kqed.org/mindshift/32503/how-the-power-of-interest-drives-learning.

Ritchhart, Ron, and David Perkins. 2008. "Making Thinking Visible." *Educational Leadership* 65 (5): 57–61.

Vygotsky, L. S. 2004. "Imagination and Creativity in Childhood." *Journal of Russian and East European Psychology* 42 (1): 7–97.